SPACE IN MOTION

Juan Goytisolo

SPACE IN MOTION

Translated by Helen R. Lane

Lumen Books

Acknowledgements

The following essays originally appeared in the following publications: "Sir Richard Burton, peregrino y sexólogo" and "Flaubert en Oriente" in *Crónicas Sarracinas*, Editorial Ruedo Ibérico: Madrid, 1982. "Las cruces de Yeste," "El museo Dillinger," "Vivir in Turquía," "La Chanca 20 años después," in *El País*; "Berliner Chronik" and "El crimen fue en Port-Bou" in *El País* and SITES; "Por qué he escogido vivir en Paris" in *Voces* and SITES; "Modesta proposición a las príncipes de nuestra bella sociedad de consumo" in *Triunfo*.

Lumen Books
446 West 20 Street
New York, NY 10011

Lumen Books are produced by Lumen, Inc., a tax-exempt, non-profit organization providing design and editorial services to other non-profit agencies. This publication is made possible in part, with public funds from the New York State Council on the Arts, the National Endowment for the Arts, and with private contributions.

Contents

Introduction

The proverbial difficulty of describing what space engenders can be obviated only by resorting to the verbal alchemy of the poet: a deceptively limitless territory, resistant to the neatly aligned syntax of ordinary speech, it requires sharp breaks, abrupt fractures, shortcuts, knowledge of the ways of rivers, seas, mountains, a patient labor of adaptation to its ever-shifting desert configuration. An undertaking with no particular perils, given our minuscule spherical shape. As mere tiny balls doomed to circle endlessly, to trace ellipses, to return, inevitably, to precisely the place where we started, our one recourse is to call upon jagged, incandescent language, ellipsoidal imagery, the elliptical lightning-flash statement. Hence the notion of space as captured in writing contains within itself, at least implicitly, the dizzying idea of motion.

From the Renaissance on, European narrative has endeavored to account for our dreams or our desires of discovery, of conquest: domesticating the exotic, exhuming the archaic, bringing to light the powerful fascination for splendid, sleeping civilizations. From the free-floating hallucination of Eldorado to the mental mirages of the chroniclers of the Indies, from the gaudy fantasies of those bedazzled by the East to the picturesque local color of the *roman des pays chauds,* the writer has tried to encompass the supposedly incommensurable: that universal earthquake whose secret epicenter was located, unbeknown to him, within the circumference of his very own writing. The "education through travel" so popular with the Romantics was subsequently to become no more than a pleasant diversion of the poet-as-nomad, the poet-as-world-wanderer — an outward, parallel representation of the miraculous power of literature.

Today we have a clear and precise idea of the limits reached by avarice on our planet. Colonialism, slavery, wars, forced or voluntary emigrations, ubiquitous travel agencies have done away with distances, coated the world with a uniform varnish of European and American fashions, styles of dress, manners and mores, spawned Arab markets, Caribbean or African villages, Turkish settlements in the heart of Paris, New York, or Berlin, blurred the boundaries of exoticism, exposed "superior" civilizations to the contamination of the "backward" ones and vice versa, created new styles of art and life based on racial intermingling, bastardization, promiscuity. The errant poet of our day experiences his space in perpetual motion, the tremors and vibration of his orbit,

1

seated at his work desk, clutching his pen or his ball-point, staring at the blank sheet of paper before him. His writing is an epicenter, a focus of contagion of impulses, exorcisms, dreams, the levitation or the alluring decoy of an elusive otherness. If the work does not infect us, that means that its author is not an authentic sick man, or else that we, his readers, have at some point in the past been inoculated against the troublesome virus of his text. In either case, our best course is to throw his book away, as an object of no use to us: the benign harmlessness of what he has written, or else our lamentable iron constitution, does not, to our misfortune, invite us to undergo the illness and the adventure of travel.

Flaubert in the Orient[1]

In December of 1975 I signed up, for the first and probably the last time in my life, for a guided tour organized by a travel agency: a ten-day excursion up the Nile by boat. My companions on this "adventure"—the term, naturally, is not mine; it is that used in the agency's brochures—were some forty-odd French and Belgian tourists, with whom I shared cabin and table accommodations aboard an old hulk not unlike the steamboats that once plied the Mississippi and, having been converted into floating casinos, are now languishing away at dockside in St. Louis or New Orleans. It is irrelevant to my purpose here to dwell on what was most impressive about the trip: the splendid skies, the Nubian temples, the journey through one of the most beautiful and moving landscapes in the world. I shall limit myself to summing up the reactions of my travel companions, which I carefully noted down day after day all during the unforgettable, exasperating trip.

My fellow passengers fell, *grosso modo*, into two categories: the "cultured" ones, or, to be more precise, the ones eager to absorb "culture"; and the ones who, by reason of their visible disdain for ancient art, we may call the "ignorant." The former spent their days with their noses buried in the thumbnail historical run-downs in Nagel, Fodor, or the Guide Bleu; they looked at, though they did not see, the monuments described in their travel books; they absorbed, like attentive students, the resounding erudition of a cicerone, who to all appearances was reciting from memory the endless chronology of pharoahs and their dynasties. The latter group yawned with boredom on excursions and visits ashore, complained constantly of the discomforts of the cruise, the monotony of the meals on board, their catastrophic effects, the continual, irksome problems created by the inadequate water pressure in the heads.

Both groups admired the majestic beauty of the country. For both, however, it served merely as a term of comparison, the other term being their low, not to say abysmal, opinion of its inhabitants. The latter were, at best, *de braves Arabes*, an expres-

---

[1]In both French and Spanish, the terms "Orient" and "Oriental" may refer to the East in general; to those countries east of the Mediterranean or the ancient Roman empire; or to Asiatic countries in general. They are also often used to refer to the Islamic countries in Africa and the Near and Middle East. I here follow the author's use of the word, usually in the latter sense, with occasional specific modifiers. (*Translator's Note.*)

sion that applied only to *fellahin* contemplated from a distance. Normally, physical proximity and any attempt on the part of such individuals to secure a gratuity in exchange for some dubious service rendered immediately placed them in the category of *pauvres diables*. Their continual plea for *baksheesh* (a tip, a contribution in the name of charity) aroused a unanimous reaction of rejection: people completely lacking in dignity. One of our number, a former civil servant of her country, now retired, whose heart unfailingly went out to donkeys (*oh, les petits ânes!*), exclaimed on a certain memorable occasion: *"Eux, au moins, ne demandent pas des bakshich!"*

The "cultured" and the "ignorant" alike threw themselves, with only two or three honorable exceptions, into the game of clichés and hoary epithets. Needless to say, these stereotyped judgments of character were invariably negative and very often insulting: lazy, whiningly persistent, unreliable, dirty, backward, servile. The "natives" were never seen as individuals or as human beings, only as constituents of a shapeless mass, devoid of personality or features differentiating one from another: simply Moslems, Arabs, Middle-Easterners. Members of some strange, opaque, inscrutable tribe, not creatures of flesh and blood, our fellows. If circumstances in the country had been other than they were at that time, if a sudden revolution had shaken them from their "lethargy," the simplifications would naturally have taken the form of the sort of pat phrases we hear applied today to Iranians and Palestinians: fanaticism, cruelty, terror, screaming masses—always masses. As is obvious, such hackneyed expressions and cut-and-dried generalizations have no objective validity whatsoever: if they reveal anything at all, it is the ethnocentric and at times openly racist prejudices of those who resort to them. Clichés of this sort do not portray or characterize the "natives"; they portray and mirror those who mouth them.

From the first compendiums and treatises describing the Orient published in the eighteenth century, the authors did their best to domesticate and encompass the immensity of the subject by systematically resorting to formulas and definitions whose aim was to bare the secrets of the "mysterious East" to the European reader. Mastering the arcana of the culture of the Orient was the best possible means of mastering the Orient itself: once it had been described, analyzed, expounded, condensed—subjected, in a word, to a sort of vivisection—the European powers, with their armadas and their expeditionary corps, could arrogate to themselves the right to take it over, to dispose of it as they pleased. Just as the failure of American Indians to exploit their natural resources legitimized intervention (all Europeans ever do is "intervene": they do not attack, sack, enslave, or exterminate "natives") by the colonial powers, so the ignorance and abandonment of their own age-old Afroasiatic cultures by the indigenous peoples of the area justifed their being "taken in hand" by those who, in view of their superior knowledge of them, of their past, their present, their future, and their aspirations, were naturally entitled to, and exercised, the wholly beneficent role of guardian and tutor. The thorough pillaging of the works of art of Middle Eastern civilizations in order to enrich the collections of the Louvre or of the British Museum announced the advent of colonial armies and of colonial administrations: it also served as the intellectual and moral guarantee of the more exalted rank of the latter in the human hierarchy. The Orient as catalogued in books and museums became the legal property of an Occident superior in every respect, more cultivated, better programmed.

Edward W. Said has set forth most convincingly the different phases of the process of appropriation of the Near East undertaken by Orientalists: from the descriptions, histories, and travel books of Abbot Le Mascrier, the Count of Volney, and Dr. Lane to the works of Renan, Sacy, Palmer, Dozy, Muir. The ever-increasing Anglo-French intervention in "indigenous" affairs, the broadening of commercial ties, the influx of visitors spur the publication of the first guidebooks. Predictably, as happens with every literary genre that comes to embrace a set of formal rules and acquires a set of formal characteristics, the texts support each other, feed on each other: their relationship to the corpus of previous works is invariably closer and stronger than the one that links them to reality. Simplifications, clichés, stereotypes are handed down from generation to generation, constituting an inheritance that seems to be transmitted by solemn testamentary covenant. On the one hand, the "mystery of the Orient," its strangeness, its exoticism, its enigma, its unfathomable arcana; on the other, its familiar ineradicable vices: cruelty, laziness, corruption, inability to change for the better, sexual licence, lack of exactitude, fanatical turn of mind. The deleterious influence of cheap colored Oriental chromos[2] becomes evident very early on: because of it, direct experience is subjected to the acid test of the cliché, and the latter inevitably wins out. Travelers and future writers arrived in the Near East and the Maghreb with entirely

---

[2]In a magnificent recent text, accompanying a series of nineteenth-century post-cards picturing the Orient as seen through the colonizer's eyes, the Algerian poet Malek Alloula analyzes the extravagant European fantasies surrounding the Oriental bordello. See *Le harem colonial*, Paris-Genève, 1981.

preconceived ideas, knowing beforehand the descriptions, histories, and travel books of what they were about to see, what they were about to think. The résumés of the guidebooks cancel out the errors and the shortcomings of personal vision. The best interpretation of reality is to be found in books. To write about reality is to exercise that hallowed function of the copyist known as plagiarism. This is as true of authors today as of those who, throughout the nineteenth century, portrayed Oriental manners and customs. As Rouger and Auriant have proved, many of Gérard de Nerval's descriptions in his *Voyage en Orient* and his *Les femmes du Caire* are copied straight out of Lane's celebrated guidebook. More notable and more significant still: when Marx visits Algiers in the last years of his life and describes the panorama of Algiers, the appearance of its inhabitants, or the plants in the Jardin d'Essai to Engels or to his daughters Jenny and Laura, his letters reproduce line for line entire passages from the "Itinéraire de l'Algérie" of a long-forgotten precursor of today's famed Guide Bleu: the Guide-Joanne. Pierre Enckell, to whom we owe this titillating discovery,[3] rightfully comments: "What is interesting about this anecdote is the almost systematic refusal of direct observation, the need to depend on written documents to recount personal experiences." If someone of the stature of Marx—out of a lack of confidence in his gifts of observation, laziness, or a lack of sympathy for the subject—subjected his own vision to the authority of a text that had become canonical, it would naturally be presumptuous of me to reproach my travel companions on the Nile excursion for having constantly resorted to stereotyped concepts and criteria to describe the "natives."

When, as a consequence of the adverse opinion of his friends Louis Bouilhet and Maxime Du Camp regarding the draft of his *La tentation de saint Antoine*, Flaubert abandons his literary projects and shelves the book, he decides, in order to console himself, to realize his long-standing dream of journeying to the Orient and boards a ship bound for Egypt. The idea of visiting the very sources of the culture of antiquity was in no way a novel one: Chateaubriand, Lamartine, Nerval, among others, had set out in that direction before him, in search of a creative vision, a sense of identity, the living out of religious or erotic fantasies, a satisfaction of the hunger for local color. The "journey to the Orient," as popularized by the Romantic writers, had made a pilgrimage to Syria, Egypt, or Constantinople a must for literati, in somewhat

[3]See "Un plagiat touristique signé Karl Marx," *Les Nouvelles Littéraires*, 19 juillet 1979.

the same way that the "beat" phenomenon would later launch a mass escape to India, Afghanistan, or Nepal. For a series of cultural and political reasons, the contact with the Orient had come to be regarded as one of the essential experiences in the spiritual education of the man of letters. The Orient was valued not so much in and for itself as for the fact that it gave rise to a literary vocation or allowed one to jell: in other words, because it held promise of having a possible bearing on the creative process of the writer.[4]

Like those in whose footsteps he was following, Flaubert had assimilated the subject beforehand, thanks to an already extensive Orientalist bibliography that enjoyed unquestioned authority. But what little by little distinguished his letters with their minutely detailed account of his itinerary from the travel notes of others before him is the fact that his interests in the journey that he was undertaking were less those of an artist in the bud, eager to accumulate experience and information useful for his future *oeuvre*, than they were those of a curious and skeptical bourgeois, eager to enjoy the privileges automatically conferred on him by his ethnic, class, and national background. If I may be permitted the anachronism, these origins make him more akin to my travel companions on the Nile excursion than to the bearded youngsters of Delhi, Kabul, or Katmandu. While I do not wish to deal here with the subject in exhaustive detail, I shall reproduce a few examples to illustrate my point; they are taken from his *Lettres d'Égypte*, edited by Antoine Naaman.

On arriving in Alexandria, the first thing he spies on the dock is a group of "*braves Arabes* fishing with pole and line in the most serene manner imaginable." Having reached Cairo, he observes that his compatriots, and Christians in general, occupy the highest posts in government and on the social ladder, so that the "*pauvres diables d'Arabes* never know who it is that they may be dealing with and bow to any and every European frock coat just to be on the safe side." The vision provided by the authentic text—the East as condensed in guidebooks for cultivated tourists—orients his spatial and human perceptions from the start: "You ask me if the East comes up to my expectations. It does indeed, and is even

---

[4]Nerval's vision is steeped in preconceived Orientalist images. On spying veiled women for the first time, he exclaims: *Me voilà en pleines Mille et Une Nuits!* ("I've stepped into The Thousand and One Nights!") The same clichés of odalisques and harem fantasies crop up frequently in Balzac's narratives, especially in his celebrated *La fille aux yeux d'or* (*The Girl with the Golden Eyes*). See on this subject Moënis and Taha Hussein, *Présence de l'Islam dans la littérature romantique en France*.

vaster than what I had imagined. What was nebulous to me now stands out in sharp outline. Fact is supplanted by presentiment, and hence it frequently seems to me that I am suddenly rediscovering old forgotten dreams," he writes to his mother. His attitude toward the "natives" is, to put it briefly, a surprising mixture: part colonial settler and part *gentil membre* of the Club Méditerranée.

Almost the moment he has installed himself in the capital, he becomes aware of the enormous advantages that his financial means and his nationality procure him and unblushingly makes the most of them: "We will not wear Egyptian dress on the Nile. Since European attire is more respected, that is how we shall continue to dress," he writes his mother. His reactions to the pomp and circumstance with which he is received by the authorities by reason of his official mission are the typical reactions of the guest at those hotel complexes of the Third World conceived to resemble Oriental palaces, in which, for a sum of money within the reach of the pocketbook of the *petit blanc*, the latter may allow himself the luxury of feeling superior to the *pauvres diables*, and for the space of a few days live an air-conditioned dream worthy of *The Thousand and One Nights*: "The manner in which we are being received here is incredible. All joking aside, we are being treated like princes. Sassetti keeps repeating: 'I'm going to be able to say that for at least once in my life I had ten slaves to do my bidding and one who chased flies away.'" Like the future purchasers of "cheap sun," he will be offered a real banquet consisting of thirty different dishes: "One eats five or six mouthfuls of each one, whereupon another one is brought immediately." As his boat proceeds up the Nile, the "natives" dive into the river bare naked and swim out shouting: "*batchis, batchis [sic]*, Christian sirs!" On describing the scene—closely resembling the one which I had the misfortune to witness one hundred twenty-five years later and which led some of my travel companions to toss handfuls of coins and crusts of bread into the water, sometimes as far away as they could throw them, "because that way they'll deserve them"—Flaubert merely comments: "If they weren't beaten off now and again, we would be boarded by so many of them that this old hulk would be in danger of sinking."

The stereotypes forged by the Orientalists—servility, cruelty, corruption—compose a picture full of local color: "The timeworn comic effect of the slave who gets a thorough thrashing, of the brusque marketer of women, of the crafty merchant is here spontaneous, authentic, utterly delightful." The Egyptians hand out drubbings with "sublime prodigality." To escape the blows dealt them by Flaubert's and Du Camp's servants, the unhappy possessor of a basket of dates takes refuge in the sea. "Nothing could be more amusing than the sight of that black backside amid the white waves. The man was howling like a wild beast. We stood there watching, laughing our heads off. My sides still ache just thinking about it." After describing a number of incidents of this sort, Flaubert concludes, with apparent impassive objectivity: "*Batchis* and the cudgel are the fundamental reality of the Arab; one hears and sees nothing else." The bromide of the carrot and the stick, which his words exemplify, was to become more and more common currency, the very sum and substance of the "great colonial adventure."

Flaubert's letters to Bouilhet contain a veritable catalogue of street obscenities and *bizarres jouissances*. One of the deckhands on the old junker dances naked, "a lascivious dance that consisted of trying to screw himself"; to scare off some of the curious monks, he flaunts "his member and his asshole, pretending to piss and shit on their heads." A little boy of seven or eight says to the Frenchman: "Give me five *paras* so I can eat honey in honor of the prophet and I'll bring you my mother to fuck." Like his friend Du Camp, Flaubert has come to Egypt in search of "free" and above all "cheap" sex. Their threefold status as males, Europeans, and bourgeois allows them to choose whatever they please, whatever appeals to them. At no time do they ponder the question of whether the "natives" are in the same position to bargain as they: whether their "free sex" is not perhaps a lifelong curse on the heads of the young girls or the prostitutes they bed. The "delicious corruption" and natural degradation of Orientals banish all scruples and legitimize their eagerness to collect experiences: "We had scarcely set foot ashore when that disgusting lecher of a Du Camp got all excited at the sight of a black woman who was drawing water from a well. Little black boys got him just as worked up. I'd really like to know who, or rather what, doesn't make him hot!" In Esneh, Flaubert pens a magnificent description of his first night with Kuchuk Hanem: "I sucked her furiously; her body was wet with sweat, she was cold, the dance had exhausted her. . . . Contemplating this lovely sleeping creature who was snoring with her head cradled on my arm, I thought . . . of her dance, of the voice in which she sang verses, words that to me were meaningless and indistinguishable"; on returning to the city, Flaubert finds her changed (she has been ill and does not experience the same ardor as before): "I gazed at her for a long time in order to engrave her image deeply in my mind. When I left, I told her that we would return the following day, and we did not return. I confess I tasted the bitterness of all that." But outside of this sad reflection in the bulletins on the subject sent to

Bouilhet, Flaubert does not readily yield to the temptation of shallow sentimentality and self-complacency: "I fucked three women and shot my wad four times—three times before lunch and the fourth after dessert. I proposed a passage at arms to the madame herself; but as I had disdained her in the beginning, so she now turned me down cold. Too bad: I would have liked to have this full bloom to crown my work and make me think well of myself. Young Du Camp only got off once. His dong ached from a dose of the clap he caught in Alexandria from a Walachian whore. What's more, the Turkish women were scandalized by my indecency when I rinsed my cock off in full view of everyone."

Unlike the majority of travelers in the Orient and the Islamic world, Flaubert accepts his superior status without the least compunction. The diffidence—or what certain people would call the shamelessness—with which he swallows the rules of a game founded on the eternal law of might makes right nonetheless has something tonic, bracing, stimulating about it. Except on one or two occasions, he never falls into what today we would term "bad faith." The world being as it is, there is nothing to do but adapt to it and try to squeeze all the juice possible from it. Orientals are mere supernumeraries in a joyous and entertaining *tableau vivant*. We are at precisely the opposite pole from a Gide, who envelops the material agents of his "revelation" in a halo of nebulous poesy. Flaubert's attitude is closer to that of a Tony Duvert when the latter deliberately provokes and shocks. A cynic to the core, Flaubert feels no need to justify himself, thereby revealing at least some measure of honesty: by his conduct he strips the colonial paternalist of all his masks, lays his ambiguous attitude bare. "In Egypt, sodomy is an accepted practice and a subject of after-dinner conversation. At times polite denials are offered, whereupon everyone insults you and you end up confessing. Since we are traveling in order to educate ourselves, and with an express mission from the government, we regarded it as our duty to practice this mode of ejaculation," he writes ironically.

Between the esthetic focus with which we tend to view alien societies and the moral prism through which we are accustomed to view our own, Flaubert does not hesitate for an instant. His vision will be purely esthetic, hedonistic, ethnocentric, without a trace of pity or sympathy for the miserable conditions in which Orientals live. This is doubtless both sad and shocking. Yet the brutal frankness and forthrightness with which he manifests his choice are in a certain sense salutary: he makes a clean break with the hypocrisy and the fake pity that Occidentals display when confronted with the hideous flaws and horrors of the Third World.

Thus, on coming across two boats loaded with black women slaves, our author cannot resist the temptation of nosing about aboard one of them and pretending to haggle over the price of a young Abyssinian girl, in order to stay a bit longer "and enjoy the spectacle, *which had its charm*" (emphasis added). In the red-light district of Kaneh, as he writes Bouilhet: "I didn't go and fuck—deliberately, purposely, so as to prolong the melancholy of this scene and allow it to penetrate more deeply within me. And so it was that I left bedazzled, a spell that lingers still. There is nothing more beautiful than those women beckoning to you. If I had fucked, another image would have been superimposed on that one and dimmed its splendor." Egocentrism such as that, translated into the language of a cultispeaker of the cruise organized by my travel agency—sent into ecstasy by the superb spectacle of fellahin tilling their fields—, was crystallized in the following historic phrase, which I carefully recorded in my notebook: *"Quand je regarde les gestes millénaires de ces braves gens, je sens sourdre en moi de mystérieux appels."* [5]

I have often asked myself what Flaubert's reaction would have been to the phenomenon of mass tourism as promoted by travel agencies with their Oriental itineraries. Unlike Marx, the author of *L'Éducation sentimentale* did not believe in the redeeming virtues of progress or in the historic mission of the proletariat: his unforgettable portrait of Sénécal has the merit of being that of the first specimen of the future bureaucratized leader of the working class, whose ideal, he will say, is a "virtuous democracy, at once a farm and a textile factory, a sort of American Sparta in which the individual will exist only to serve Society, more omnipotent, absolute, infallible, and divine than the Great Lamas and Nebuchadnezzars." Flaubert's historical pessimism had enabled him to foresee the deluge of vulgarity and commonness in which European civilization would drown his Orientalized Orient: our model of obligatory happiness—in which he did not believe—would be built of the very same clichés of otherness and exoticism that had led him to undertake his journey. Confronted with an almost European Constantinople, he had written, with mingled skepticism and nostalgia: "Oh, Orient, where are you? — Soon it will exist nowhere else but in the sun . . . Within a hundred years . . . the harem will collapse all by itself beneath the weight of serialized stories in the newspapers and operettas. . . . Everything is splitting apart here as at home. If you would live, live it up!"

---

[5]"When I contemplate the time-hallowed gestures of those good people, a sense of mysterious summonses wells up within me." (*Translator's Note.*)

Sir Richard Burton, Pilgrim and Sexologist

To Guillermo Cabrera Infante

The memorial edition of *Personal Narrative of a Pilgrimage to Al-Medinah and Meccah*, dedicated to "all English-speaking peoples Who respect and honor the name of RICHARD BURTON, the Soldier, Linguist, Scholar, Explorer and Discoverer, Poet, Author, and Benefactor to Science; in recognition of the labours of a long and honorable life, devoted to the Service of his Country, and to the advancement of its Knowledge and of its Literature," was published, under the supervision of his widow, some three years after the writer's death. In the copy I have at hand—beautifully reprinted with the original engravings and maps by Dover Publications (New York: 1964)—there is a photograph of Isabel Burton, as blonde and bulky as a Germanic Valkyrie, her head covered with a white lace coif, her neck and hairy chin hidden beneath a high shirred collar, and clad in an amply-cut, dark-colored tunic that at once conceals and reveals her splendid, opulent figure; the pose shows her seated at a desk, holding an open book, as she contemplates a distant point beyond the camera lens with the inspired and affable expression of a benevolent fairy. The humanity and altruism of her sentiments appear to be incontrovertible, and the reader of the brief preface that introduces the work will read without mental reservations: "After my beloved husband had passed away from amongst us, after the funeral had taken place and I had settled in England, I began to think in what way I could honor him." An exemplary widow, after having been an exemplary wife, Isabel Burton—likewise the author of a pious hagiography of her husband, suitable for being read aloud to children in parochial schools or religious groups—nonetheless concealed within herself, among many other things, a frightening vocation as a censor, skilled in the arts of ritual burnings and the stripping of pages from manuscripts deemed culpable: once her beloved spouse was dead and gone she proceeded, as we now know, to expurgate his writings and books, consigning to the flames, "sadly and reverently," as she herself acknowledged, one page after another, not only of Burton's new version of *The Perfumed Garden*, with accompanying commentaries, that he was working on at the time of his death, but also—a fact that she did not reveal—his intimate diaries and travel notebooks, which encompassed forty years of personal experiences and reflections, systematically eliminating from his *oeuvre*—in conformity with

13

her ideal image of her husband, whom she described as the "purest, most refined and modest man who has ever lived"—every explicit reference to sex and above all to homosexuality.

The life of Captain Burton was truly extraordinary, his excellent version of *The Thousand Nights and a Night* and his essays and notes on sexual anthropology that survived the holocaust having earned him the marvelously amusing nickname of "dirty Dick."[1] Born in 1821 of a well-off, eccentric family, he roamed all through Europe from a very early age, learning on his own French, Latin, Greek, Italian, and the dialect of Naples, one after the other. In this latter city, he taught himself the arts of the sword, saber, and rapier and practiced until he had become a master of them—and the future author of a treatise on their history and handling. While still just a youngster, he took up with whores and ruffians, and on being sent up to Oxford to study divinity he surprised his fellow-students by his manners of a street tough and his imposing mustache. In university circles, he soon distinguished himself by criticizing the ridiculous Anglicized Latin of his professors, and having fallen on bad terms with them, turned to the study of Arabic, with the occasional aid of a Spaniard, Gayandos. Undisciplined by nature, incapable of adapting himself to the narrowmindedness and monotony of English life, and persuaded, in his own words, that "a man demonstrates his valour by doing as he pleases," he enlisted, at the age of twenty-two, in the army of the East India Company. Once he had arrived in Bombay, he immersed himself in learning and becoming proficient in a number of Oriental languages—his gifts as a polyglot surpassed even those of his compatriot George Henry Borrow, with whom, moreover, he had a great many other things in common—, and after obtaining a certificate as an interpreter in seven languages (he was later to master twenty-nine different tongues)—he was signed on by the British High Command in the campaign against the Sikhs. His passionate interest in the life and customs of Indian peoples led him to dress and live as they did, passing himself off as a merchant and healer named Mirza Abdullah and thereby collecting a series of first-hand data as to their social norms, beliefs, taboos, and habits. Convinced, rightly, that the best way of entering into contact with foreign peoples is to embark upon sexual

---

[1]Among the biographies of Burton that I have consulted, some of them favorable and others hostile to his wife, the one that is most interesting, trustworthy, and complete is undoubtedly that of Fawn M. Brodie, entitled *The Devil Drives* (New York: 1967). A number of the episodes and anecdotes recounted below I have also taken from Byron Farwell.

relations with them, his taste for such adventures—which had already manifested itself in his adolesence when he had taken up with a gypsy girl—earned him the opprobrium of his comrades-at-arms for whom the atypical Burton was nothing but a "white nigger." It is certain fact that the young officer did not behave according to any of the established rules: he not only wore Oriental dress, dyed his face with henna, and partook of *bhang* with addicts thereof, but also studied the language of simians, kept half a dozen of them in his house, and went out for walks accompanied by a female monkey adorned with pearl earrings, whom he introduced to everyone as his wife. To explain his accent, he claimed that he was half Arab and half Persian, just as Ali Bey,[2] in Morocco, passed himself off as Syrian. This fondness for disguises—for frequently shifting roles in the "Oriental scene"—no doubt betrayed an ambiguity in his relations with others of which he may not have been entirely conscious. His love of practical jokes and pranks was lifelong, causing him countless problems and making him many enemies. In order to dupe professional scholars and archaeologists—to the very end of his life his hatred of the university Establishment was undying—he forged a document that "proved" that one of the lost tribes of Israel had made its way to the Indus valley, and "unearthed" at an excavation site an Etruscan jar that he himself owned, thereby persuading specialists that the Etruscans had originally come from Sind. But what did his career irreparable harm was his overstepping all the bounds of "decency" and providing Sir Charles Napier, the governor of India, with a detailed report on the brothels and ephebes and transvestites in Karachi: despite its confidential nature, his learned technical paper on the subject was purposely transmitted to the Government and, as the reader can readily imagine, it caused a scandal. Burton did not receive the promotion that his merits and aspirations should rightfully have earned him, and after recovering from a mild attack of cholera, he returned to England, where he proposed to the Royal Geographical Society a plan for exploring the Arab peninsula, including zones that no Occidental was to set foot in for another eighty years. Confronted by the refusal of the East India Company, to whose army he was still attached, to extend the leave he had been granted, Burton cur-

---

[2]In 1814 Domingo Badía, a self-taught Arabist from Barcelona, published in French a volume entitled *Voyages d'Ali Bey en Afrique et en Asie,* a pseudonymous account of his travels throughout the Middle East and his pilgrimages to Mecca disguised as a great Arab sheik and descendant of the Prophet. See Juan Goytisolo's *Crónicas sarracinas* (Ruedo Ibérico, 1981), Chapter 6, for details. *(Translator's Note.)*

tailed his travel plans, limiting them to the visit of the sacred cities of Islam. In 1852, again disguised as Mirza Abdullah, he took off for Alexandria, following in the footsteps of Ali Bey. From his travels in Egypt and Arabia there resulted the manuscript of *Personal Narrative*, written when he rejoined his regiment in Bombay—one of the classics of English travel literature.

Burton's account of his Moslem pilgrimage is undoubtedly his masterwork, and a book that crowns a series of works by others on the subject, the fruit of personal experiences, observations, and commentaries of supposed believers in the religion of Islam. Beginning with Dr. John Wilson's attacks on Ali Bey for "his unjustifiable and capricious disguise as a Mohammedan pilgrim," numerous writers, both European and Arab, have pilloried, for religious and moral reasons, the device of passing oneself off as a pilgrim, condemning it by turn as an act of bad faith, blasphemy, and hypocrisy. "To feign to be a practitioner of a religion in which the adventurer himself does not believe, to execute with scrupulous exactitude, as acts of the greatest and most sacred importance, ceremonies which he inwardly ridicules and proposes in turn to ridicule before others, to turn for weeks and months the most noble and solemn gestures of man toward his Maker into a deliberate, base pantomime, not to mention other even more sordid points—all that appears to be scarcely compatible with the character of a European gentleman and less still of a Christian," one of them writes. For reasons that for the most part are well-founded, recent authors have also dealt harshly with the claims of certain travelers and anthropologists that they are gathering information or scientific data when, like Burton, they pass on their knowledge and findings about the Orient to their fellow-countrymen and not to Orientals, thereby making these latter merely the object of a humanistic and ethnological discourse in which they are not invited to participate, its real audience inevitably being the public of the West. All this is true, and I have dealt with the subject on other occasions, but above and beyond the fact that it is very difficult to keep from being influenced by the ideas embodied by the historical dynamics of a given era—as the example of Marx himself proves—, a number of the criticisms leveled against Burton do not strike me in his case as being either factually accurate or impartial.

To a European of the middle of the nineteenth century, the role played by English imperialism in furthering progress in the Near East and in India was evident—as evident as that played by the new Russia in its Asiatic colonies was to a Communist after 1917. The concept of ethnocentrism is fairly recent, and none of the great thinkers or revolutionaries of the past century wholly escapes being charged with it. In some cases, the pseudo-Abdullah does indeed adopt the point of view of an Englishman, convinced that the worldwide expansion of his country is the product of an irresistible historical current, and therefore advises the British authorities, for instance, to send a consul to Al-Hijaz, until the day comes when, as he puts it, "the tide of events forces us to occupy the mother-city of Al-Islam." But just as Marx, on emphasizing the beneficial nature of the English colonization of India, reveals the injustices of the colonizing power and sensitizes us to them, Burton, in spite of, or rather because of his functions in the British administrative machine, clearsightedly sounds the warning that sooner or later Asiatics will discover that his compatriots are not just or generous or civilized, but, on the contrary, crafty rogues, that English officials accept bribes and have recourse to oppressive methods; when that time comes, Asiatics will then contemplate the possibility of a Saint Bartholomew's Day in the East. "Everyone knows," he writes, "that if the people of India could be unanimous for a day they might sweep us from their country as dust before a whirlwind."[3]

The works written by travelers in the Islamic world are particularly steeped in the many Orientalist stereotypes that have shaped European thought in recent centuries. Burton is no exception to that rule, but the clichés and commonplaces that we find in his pages are of little moment if we compare them with his extremely acute observations and his first-hand accounts of every country he visits. Every so often he admittedly falls into those generalizations and trivialities in the manner of Ortega y Gasset, Keyserling, or André Maurois that Orientalists find so captivating, but even though these defects partially justify the criticism of Burton's book by Edward Said and other Arab authors, it nonetheless cannot be reduced to this sort of writing: far from it. Although his facts and commentaries about Moslems are meant for a Western public, certain of them are of interest to Moslems as well, inasmuch as what he has to say about them allows them to see themselves from outside and thereby to further their knowledge of themselves. Curiosity based on genuine human sympathy, a sense of self-criticism, the ability to question the fundamental tenets of

---

[3]Despite his official duties in the Foreign Office, Burton maintained his anticolonialist opinions to the end: he was persuaded that England should keep out of Africa, and in his satirical poem "Stone Talk" he called the great conquerors of India bandits who had brought misery and damnation with them to the Asian subcontinent. Concerned about the harm it might do his career, Isabel secretly bought up the entire limited edition and—a foretaste of the grand burning of 1890—completely destroyed every copy.

received tradition are universally valid qualities, and the Arab reader can enrich himself through them and compensate for certain lacunae owed in large part to a defensive attitude and an arrogance that are fairly comprehensible when viewed within their historical context, yet are extremely harmful. The act of penetrating to the very foundations of other cultures and societies is an inalienable right of the human mind, and to maintain that the presuppositions and the framework of beliefs of a particular civilization can be analyzed only by someone who identifies fully with them and is therefore not subject to uncertainties and doubts would be as absurd and as sterile as to claim that only a Catholic can write about Catholics, a Chinese about the Chinese, and a woman about women. While ethnocentrism, by passing the values of others through its own filter in a way that is absolute and incontestable, is to be condemned, a radically opposed position— that of impugning the validity of a critical examination of a culture by someone situated outside it—would deny the fruitfulness of cultural interchanges and lead to a compartmentalization and an isolation both deadly and impossible to maintain. The gaze of the intruder who is not blind to his surroundings or wearing blinkers cannot be reduced to a pure and simple violation of the religious sentiments of others. Even though, unlike Ali Bey, Burton sheds his "cover" as a pilgrim on beginning the account of his travels and with it the fiction of his belief in the dogmas of the Moslem faith, his reflections on the latter give proof of great understanding and respect, and he does not fall into the contradictions or anachronisms that sometimes pepper the Barcelona traveler's pages. In his description of certain rites of the pilgrimage— the stoning of the devil, etc.—he does not fail to mention their superstitious nature, but what nation, either in the Orient or in Europe, he observes, has been able as yet to exorcise every last shadow or suspicion of idolatry from its ceremonies? He adds that in England, Brittany, Ireland, and Italy, he was present at similar rituals, which apparently were not at all shocking to those who would not hesitate to denounce to high heaven any and every manifestation of "Moslem fanaticism." Islamic liturgy is far more austere than the Catholic and it does not attempt to intimidate or seduce as the latter does: " . . . at Meccah," he says, "there is nothing theatrical, nothing that suggests the opera; but all is simple and impressive." In general, Burton's observations with regard to beliefs are an amalgam of his rationalistic criticism of religious liturgy—Islamic as well as Anglican or Catholic—and a receptive and open attitude toward the alien faith, free of paternalism and ill-will. As with Badía, in the end the profound belief of Moslems inspires his respect and even fills him with emotion.

"I have seen the religious ceremonies of many lands," he avows, "but never—nowhere—aught so solemn, so impressive as this."

A comparison of his attitude and Flaubert's is quite revealing in this respect. While the French novelist embarks for Alexandria filled with pride at his superiority as a cultivated bourgeois and resolved to enjoy his privileges and material means to the fullest, to the point that he gives up his Oriental finery when he realizes that European dress earns him greater respect from the Arabs, the English official pursues precisely the opposite course: fleeing the society of the army officers and civil servants of his country, he immediately endeavors to mingle with Asiatics, learns their languages, follows their norms and customs, avoids the distance that a uniform creates, feels most comfortable when relations are direct and straightforward, rejects the advantages of the *sahib*. Whereas Flaubert—like the majority of French writers of the period who journeyed through the Orient and Spain—turns into a representative of and spokesman for the values of his native land with that chauvinism, condescension, and pretentiousness so common in his compatriots (although in his case he does so with just a touch of irony), Burton—like Borrow, T. E. Lawrence, or Gerald Brenan—maintains ties with his country that are contradictory and confused, lacking a center, so to speak. His youthful wanderings all over the continent of Europe, he says, were responsible for the fact that neither he nor his brother ever managed to understand English society fully, nor did that society in turn understand them. English without wanting to be, as Cernuda would say, Burton finds England the only country in which he ever feels at home. Everything in it seems small, miserable, ugly to him: its middle-class front gardens strike him as minuscule, as though they had been sold by the inch; the desperate cleanliness and spick-and-span polish of its houses fill him with loathing; the air of its cities suffocates him; the gloomy and self-absorbed expressions of its inhabitants haunt him like a vision of Judgment Day. He makes the journey to Egypt, on his way to Mecca, "thoroughly tired of 'progress' and of 'civilization.' " For this reason, he sedulously avoids contact with Westernized Arabs who talk of European politics, sit in armchairs, eat with a fork, profess to admire liberal ideas: "and was I not flying from such things?" he exclaims. His gnawing inner discontent with his homeland and its people, his disdain for the arrogance that invariably causes the most uncultured and stupid Englishman to believe himself capable of governing a million "natives," his amazing openness and ability to adapt to the lives of all groups and races confer a wholesome relativity upon his judgments, freeing them of the dead weight of any sort of dogmatism.

Moreover, his Oriental disguise is not motivated by the conceited and narcissistic impulses of a Badía. The Barcelona "pilgrim" uses his to enhance his social status and cloak himself in a prestige that neither his origins nor his talent have earned him in his own country. Burton, however, seeks to command attention and respect by his conduct, not by his attire. This lowers others' esteem for him, but what he loses in easy opportunities and vainglory he gains in knowledge of his neighbor and of himself. The limited resources he has at his disposal to complete the pilgrimage oblige him to put his courage, proficiency, cleverness to the test. His fascination for disguise no doubt stemmed from an inner discontent and perhaps also represented a repudiation of the world of officialdom, which consistently ignored his exceptional intelligence and gifts. We might even be inclined to believe that at times it also had fetishistic connotations, though without the exhibitionism in this regard that the author of *The Seven Pillars of Wisdom* would glory in at a later date.

When he leaves Southampton in 1853, Burton is already dressed in the attire of his *alter ego* Mirza Abdullah. In order to pursue his anthropological aims, he has decided to combine the attributes of a dervish and those of a healer: if the former offer him the advantages of irresponsibility and secrecy, the latter will be of great use in enabling him to work his way into the very warp and woof of society and enter into contact with the opposite sex. His looks and build are of enormous help in successfully perpetrating this imposture. Isabel describes him at about this time as being "five feet eleven inches in height, very broad, thin, muscular: he had very dark hair, black, clearly defined, sagacious eyebrows; a brown, weather-beaten complexion; straight Arab features; a determined looking mouth and chin, nearly covered by an enormous black moustache. . . ." With his skull shaved and his face dyed with walnut juice to make up for the niggardliness and feebleness of the British sun—a recipe that he immediately dispenses with once he has acquired a tan—, he is perfect in the role and successfully passes the silent scrutiny of servants, the curious, and visitors. In Cairo he discovers that his role as a dervish of Persian orgin is counterproductive: the Egyptians think less of him, and during his visit to the holy places of Arabia he runs the risk of being thrashed and humiliated by the Bedouins. He therefore returns to his earlier character part, that of an Indian Pathan, of Afghan origin, whose knowledge of Persian and Arabic are presumably the fruit of his continual travels: a personage sufficiently complex to escape all detection by any inquisitive supposed compatriot and justify his possible inexactitudes and anachronisms.

In Egypt, Sheik Abdullah lives the life of a modest Middle Eastern healer and comes to know the "delights" of bureaucratic red tape: the description of his efforts to obtain an exit permit, going from one office to another, from doorkeeper to doorkeeper and guard to guard, only to find himself, after an endless series of waits, absurd requirements, erroneous information, and attempts at bribery, at exactly the point where he started, might be applied, without changing a single comma, to similar episodes that I have endured or witnessed in various Arab countries. In order to deal with functionaries, Burton observes, it is necessary to follow one of these three paths: bribing them, intimidating them, or importuning them with dogged perseverance—although the third approach depends entirely on luck and generally is of little use. Like him, I have run into petty office clerks made of stone, embedded in their seats and almost in symbiosis with them, speaking a language which appears to be restricted to "No," "There is no such thing," "I don't know," or "Come back tomorrow," phrases invariably uttered with no facial expression or gesture whatsoever outside the minimum movement of the tongue absolutely necessary for their articulation: an experience doubtless unknown to those travelers such as Ali Bey and Flaubert who travel encased in a cocoon. Burton relishes this sort of situation, and when a European insults him in the street because he has accidentally brushed the man with his elbow, instead of giving the fellow his just desserts, he takes the affront as a splendid compliment paid his disguise. His resorting to this masquerade does not stem only from the needs of his undertaking: disguises are an old habit with him, almost a second nature. On his return to Cairo, the brand-new *hajji*—the pilgrim who has made the journey to Mecca—cannot bring himself to doff his attire and amuses himself by wearing it as he walks past his fellow-officers at Shepheard's Hotel—without their recognizing him, naturally. When he rejoins his unit, he is still proudly flaunting his Mecca robes and his green pilgrim's turban, and on being sent on a new mission by the directors of the Company, boards ship for Aden dressed in his beloved Arab apparel.

In India, Burton has realized that though his comrades know how to make themselves obeyed, they are totally ignorant of the life, feelings, and ideas of Asiatics. In order to attain a perfect knowledge of Moslems, he diligently brackets off his own personality for the duration of the pilgrimage. When Lawrence speaks of his own efforts to imitate the mental structure of the Arabs and abandon his English self, in a certain sense he is pursuing the same aim as his predecessor and compatriot, notwithstanding the notable differences in temperament and character between them. The two of them felt the same fascination for Islam and the rough and austere universe of the Bedouins, an exclusively masculine world. Both sought out the wild freedom of the desert and a hospitable and fraternal world in which there was no place for women. Burton has begun his Arab adventure weary, in his own words, of "four years' life of European effeminacy." On tracing a portrait of the character and customs of the inhabitants of Medina, he concludes that they possess, despite their defects, a capital virtue, manliness, to a far greater degree than other Oriental populations. The social structure of a Bedouin tribe obviously favors the cultivation of those values attributed to the male sex; it is a leonine society, in which the fiercest, cleverest, and boldest man completely dominates all the others: among the males of Bedouin tribes, it is the sword that lays down the law. If this contradicts our ideas regarding civilized society and moral progress, Burton, while not gainsaying these latter, adopts, as is usual with him, a somewhat ambiguous position, continually setting forth the advantages of the primitive system of organization as far as strictly individual values are concerned: the proximity of danger, the constant uncertainty of existence, the rigors of life in the desert, the practice of arms, horsemanship, raids, banditry, and pillaging accustom Bedouins to looking death in the face and preserve certain instinctive qualities that become numbed and frustrated in our civilization; a fit body, physical skill, manual aptitude are indispensable if the Bedouin is to earn his daily bread, and they offer the foreigner a stimulating spectacle of vitality. The hospitality and courtesy of the Arab nomad are a measure of the nobility of his sentiments, and those who reproach him for his insolence have offended him by their boastful manners or are physically incapable of winning his esteem. Burton cites with admiration the age-old saying of the tribes of Al-Hijaz: "We pray not, because we must drink the water of ablution; we give no alms, because we ask them; we fast not the Ramazan month, because we starve throughout the year; and we do no pilgrimage, because the world is the House of Allah."

The aristocratic hauteur of the Bedouins and their love of untrammeled independence are founded upon a free and roving life—today swept away, as we know, by the combined effect of progress, drought, and regimentation under duress, both in Arabia and in the Sahara. Manual labor, settling down in one place imply a physical and moral degradation by comparison to the lack of restraint and the heady excitement of the desert. These criteria and these tribal values, Burton observes, also persist among the inhabitants of the holy cities, in spite of their sedentary existence: the artisans and craftsmen of Mecca and Medina are outsiders and no true son of those cities would agree to do such work for anything in the world. The aristocratic pride of the Old Christian in Spain, whose origins Americo Castro has traced, might also be related to this awareness of his nobility—of being a *hijodalgo,* a son of men of worth—that shapes the personality and the conduct of the real *badauí.* The comparison is not a gratuitous one, and a man such as Burton, with his culture and gifts of observation, established it tellingly on referring to the ancestral prejudice that prevents the Bedouin from entering into matrimony with the daughter of an artisan: "Like Castilians," he writes, "they consider labour humiliating to any but a slave. . . ." So long as the brigand obeys the code of honor and the unwritten laws of chivalry, banditry and pillaging are held to be respectable and give him a feeling of moral rectitude. Naturally, the leonine society of the desert has other facets besides its positive aspects and its stupendous advantages: the misery and helplessness of the weak or those chastized by fate, who with starving faces and imploring hands assail the pilgrim, are depicted by the traveler in masterful pages, so vivid as to make almost unbearable reading. The hordes of beggars, emaciated rogues, whose long hair, filth, and squalor qualify them for charity, those who are sick and blind and crippled, sons of the holy city, who ask the believer for the sustenance that they are unable to procure for themselves, call to mind the very same images of horror that haunt the traveler today, once an airplane flight of a few hours has taken him away from a world benumbed by its artificial prosperity. Certainly Islam, as Maxime Rodinson has aptly remarked, confers an almost sacred dignity upon poverty and creates duties toward it that elevate the indignant individual to a sort of ideal throne. But Bedouin "authenticity" cannot be—nor does it deserve to be—preserved in the face of impersonal values of justice that are of universal validity, and here Burton deftly dodges the debate. Moreover, his Bedouin society seen through rose-colored glasses is exclusively a community of men; the personality of the woman and the role she plays in this community are conspicuous by their absence. This fact did not preoccupy Lawrence overmuch, but his predecessor's curiosity and interest in this subject would lead us to expect an original explanation, if not a condemnation, of such a glaring "nonpersonhood": although on the one hand Burton avoids using the standards and current values of his own culture as criteria in his examination of another, thus giving evidence of a lack of ethnocentrism that does him honor, on the other hand he does not appear to take into account the demands for cultural and social change on the part of the woman that were already making themselves felt within Islamic civilization. Siding instead with the facile criticism of advanced, liberal Europeans, he will dismiss the subject in one curt phrase: that women are "a marketable commodity" both in England and in Arabia. The difference between monogamy and polygamy is no more than a question of nuances: "As far as my limited observations go, polyandry is the only state of society in which jealousy and quarrels about the sex are the exception and not the rule of life." Despite the fact that women counted for a great deal in his life—and his prompt return to the pathetic, insufferable Isabel after each of his escapes is there to prove it—, what he was seeking in the Arab world was above all camaraderie. "El Islam . . . seems purposely to have loosened the ties between the sexes in order to strengthen the bonds which connect man and man," he writes later in *First Footsteps in East Africa*.

Like Lawrence, Burton wrote unforgettable pages on the desert and the sentiments that possess anyone who ventures far within it:

> *It is strange how the mind can be amused amid scenery that presents so few objects to occupy it. But in such a country every slight modification of form or color rivets observation: the senses are sharpened, and perceptive faculties, prone to sleep over a confused shifting of scenery, act vigorously when excited by the capability of embracing each detail. Moreover, desert views are eminently suggestive; they appeal to the future, not to the past; they arouse because they are by no means memorial. To the solitary wayfarer there is an interest in the wilderness unknown to Cape seas and Alpine glaciers, and even to the rolling prairie—the effect of continued excitement on the mind, stimulating its powers to their pitch. Above, through a sky terrible in its stainless beauty, and the splendors of a pitiless blinding glare, the Simoom caresses you like a lion with flaming breath. Around lie drifted sand heaps, upon which each puff of wind leaves its own trace in solid waves, flayed rocks, the very skeletons of mountains, and hard unbroken plains, over which he who rides is spurred by the idea that the bursting of a water skin, or the pricking of a camel's hoof, would be a certain death of torture—a haggard land, infested with wild beasts, and wilder men—a region whose very fountains murmur the warning words, "Drink and away!" What can be more exciting? what more sublime? Man's heart bounds in his breast at the thought of measuring his*

puny force with nature's might, and of emerging tri-
umphant from the trial. This explains the Arab's prov-
erb: "Voyaging is a victory."

Personal Narrative is not the testimony of yet another traveler
to the Near East. Other authors, such as Ali Bey and Burckhardt,
had described—more or less scrupulously—the ceremonies and
vicissitudes of the pilgrimage, revealing the "mysteries and arcana of the Islamic cult" to a public that eagerly devoured exoticism. But Burton was the first to transform facts into art: the
color, variety, and richness of the "Oriental scene" had never
before been captured with such plasticity, and would not be again
until the appearance of *The Seven Pillars.* The still-young lieuten-
ant of the East India Company skillfully develops the episodes
and events in which he becomes involved, gives his ups and
downs of fortune novelistic dimensions, makes his travel companions genuine characters: the description of his guide and facto-
tum, the young Mohammed, capricious, boastful, insolent, as-
tute, boisterous, meddlesome, and insufferable, gives evidence of
qualities of humor and a richness of shading that captivate and
delight the reader. Burton does not shy away from painting himself in comic and grotesque situations, nor does he fail to give an
account of his shortcomings and blunders. The long passage dealing with his alcoholic duel with the impressive Albanian captain—
a tall, wild, herculean, strong-nerved colossus, with fierce eyes,
thin lips, pointed mustachios, and a shaved skull, as tough and as
quarrelsome as the rest of his breed—is a piece of brilliant writing: the mutual fascination of the two contenders and the re-
pressed sexual desire of the Britisher (who confesses that he runs
after his excited companion, prowling through the night in search
of a chorus of dancing girls, "begging him, as a despairing wife
might urge a drunken husband to return home") subtly show
through, all during a series of rowdy comic incidents that turn the
fondak in which they are lodging upside down and irremediably
sully Burton's image as a devout pilgrim. "Throughout the Cara-
vanserai," he concludes, "nothing was talked of for nearly a
week but the wickedness of the captain of Albanian irregulars,
and the hypocrisy of the staid Indian doctor. Thus it was, gentle
reader, that I lost my reputation of being a 'serious person' at
Cairo."

Although this incident, despite its waggish tone, gives us a
glimpse of the Burton who ordinarily remains hidden behind his
meticulous and impersonal observation of the Arabs, the reader of
the book will find no voluntary revelation of his emotions or sentiments. While Lawrence, speaking of the Bedouins, continually

25

gives his feelings away, his predecessor gives proof of a great reticence in speaking of himself, as though the religious pretext of the work forbade such a thing. As we know, Burton always manifested a lively interest in the sexual life of the peoples of remote areas, but this element was carefully excluded from *Personal Narrative*. The sphere of his private life belonged to his notebooks and intimate journals, but these were burned by Isabel. In order to know anything about that life, the reader must search through notes, comments, and references scattered throughout a dozen titles, his correspondence with colleagues and friends, and above all the footnotes and the "Terminal Essay" appended to his version of *The Thousand Nights and a Night*. Works such as *Sind, The Unhappy Valley, First Footsteps in Africa, Zanzibar*, etc. bring together an extraordinary number of notes and documents on engagements, marriage rites, prostitution, sodomy, adultery, techniques of love-making, and aphrodisiac recipes that make the author of them an unquestionable pioneer in the field of modern sexual anthropology. From the moment of his arrival in India, Burton discovers that learning to play erotic games formed part of the education of children and that guidebooks for betrothed couples were obligatory reading for men and women of the upper classes: whores or not, Hindu women held Europeans in contempt for knowing nothing about the art of retention of semen and for not being able to satisfy their desires with the necessary refinements or lack of haste. He studies in minute detail the frequent infidelity of Cairo and Somali women, the use of philters and talismans by Hindustani, Persian, and Arab women, the activities of Beluchi procuresses, the punishments and executions of cuckolded husbands. In Harar, he verifies the existence not only of clitoridectomy, which Europeans had known about since antiquity, but also of the hideous ritual of infibulation, still practiced even today in the Valley of the Nile, Ethopia, and the sub-Saharan area: the cut lips of the victim's vulva are sutured together before she reaches puberty, he says, and remain so until the nuptial ceremony, and may be sewn back together again by the husbands when they go away from home or if they mistrust their wives' fidelity; the difficult consummation of the sexual act, because of the narrowness of the opening, obliges the bridegroom to augment his physical strength by a diet of meat in order to be able to forcibly penetrate the obstacle with his "sword of love": if he is unable to do so, Burton indicates, he must resort to using a knife. After such a gruesome description, the reader finds that it beggars belief to learn that these mutilated women sew and unsew their pudenda behind their husbands' backs in order to satisfy their own desires. In point of fact, our author shares the stereotypes of the era as regards the insatiable sexual appetite of Hindu, Arab, and African women, and, influenced no doubt by his reading of the *Kama Sutra* and *The Thousand Nights and a Night,* he is of the opinion that the Semite and Hindustani women of Zanzibar prefer blacks because of the extraordinary size of the latters' penises, thereby leading the women's relatives and spouses to keep them away from places where there are blacks so as to spare them bitterness and the dangers of temptation. In view of the reigning puritanism and the predictable reactions of the public—Isabel's pyromaniacal impulses were not exceptional in Victorian England—, Burton usually chose to write about such subjects in Latin; the knowledge of that language acted as a sort of diploma of morality for the readers of that day, just as the possession of a passport under Franco's rule allowed the holders of one the privilege of seeing films in the movie theaters of Perpignan that were forbidden the vulgar. After 1880, the year in which, despite the pressure and the moral blackmail to which his wife subjected him, he devoted all his time to the translation of the classics of Oriental exoticism, he adopted a series of precautions—anonymous authorship, writing under pseudonyms, false printer's colophons— that unfortunately were of no use in preventing the holocaust: the enemy, this time, was in his own home.

Although the destruction of the notebooks and intimate journals keeps us from having a thorough knowledge of Burton's private life, certain passages of works written before or after *Personal Narrative* either refer explicitly to, or at least mention in passing, amorous adventures and fuckings that escaped Isabel's puritanical zeal. Most significantly, the author scorned and carefully avoided the English women who belonged to his milieu, finding them pharisaical and cold as icicles. Outside of a few platonic attachments, his wife was the only respectable woman with whom he ever had an intimate relation, and though Burton rarely wrote about her and everything that we know about their life as a couple comes from Isabel, whose absorbing, possessive, voracious passion is set forth at length in countless pages, the reasons that moved Richard to yield to her remain enveloped in shadow. From their first fleeting meeting, the young girl feels irresistibly attracted by his virile looks, and decides that, come what may, he and he alone will be her lord and master. Other possible suitors appear to her to be vulgar and effeminate by comparison: she therefore waits four years for chance to bring them together again, devours the accounts of his travels that he writes, dreams of being his guardian angel, and follows him—the way Marlene Dietrich follows Gary Cooper in the romantic final scene of *Morocco*— across deserts and barren plains. In her eyes Captain Burton was an absolutely exceptional man—an opinion that happened to be entirely justified—whom she worshipped almost to the point of idolatry and for whom she gladly accepted all manner of trials and tribulations so long as they did not contradict her ironclad faith in God. Her diary and correspondence, included by her biographer William Henry Wilkins in *The Romance of Isabel Lady Burton*, centered on one subject and one subject only: the absent hero. He, on the contrary, manifested much more patience than enthusiasm all during their life together, though at times Isabel's childlike obstinacy and vehemence touched his heart. His prolonged celibacy, his probable need to compensate for the constant roaming about that had marked his life since earliest childhood by a stable affection, his desire to find firm anchorage in England each time he returned from his globetrotting adventures constitute a partial explanation of his decision. To it we should add what Fawn M. Brodie points out in her luminous biography of him, on speaking of the long-lasting consequences of his report on the male brothel of Karachi:

> *The faint smell of brimstone—provoked and abhorred—would follow Burton everywhere from India, the rumor that "something was known" stayed with him all his life, and none of his hundreds of words affectionately detailing the attractiveness of Oriental women would quite erase it.*

Whatever the cause of his surrender to the virginal assaults of the girl, he had barely asked for her hand when he took off on the long journey that he had been planning ever since his visit to Harar: the discovery of the sources of the Nile. The marriage did not take place until years later, after a series of incidents and delays that Isabel's naiveté—determined as she was to make of him an exemplary, respectable, Catholic man—colors with unintended humor.

For all her diligence and vigilance, the new bride could not keep her beloved Richard from savoring more varied and more tasty dishes than the pap served him at home: his works mention the existence of concubines with whom he lived in India, tell of his amorous flights with Somali women, and sing the praises of the girls of the African Wagogo tribe who graciously smile during coitus. Although his account of his experiments with Egyptian prostitutes is not as detailed and direct as Flaubert's, both brought away from their frequenting of them the very same wretched souvenir: syphilis. In general, Burton's feelings of admiration for Arabs are not extended to Africans and Hindus. Some of his descriptions of the tribes of Tanganyika, Cameroon, or Benin can even be branded as racist, and though he may envy the real or supposed virile attributes of blacks, he condemns their drunkenness, their servility, and their barbarism.[4] Having been contaminated by their contact with Africans, the Arabs of Zanzibar strike him as weak and corrupt, and the havoc wrought there by venereal diseases fills him with horror. But to the end of his days he maintained his familiarity with Moslems and his sense of identification with them and with "their respect for the body": whereas the atmosphere of Christianity "depresses and demoralizes me," he writes shortly before his death, "being amongst Moslems again is a kind of repose to me."[5]

As Isabel soon realized, her rivals most to be feared belonged to the other sex. Though the scandal of the Karachi brothel report had more or less quieted down, the *non sanctas* friendships of her husband, his fondness for expeditions and groups composed solely of males, and a number of the notes and comments in his travel books began to cause her increasing anxiety concerning Richard's hidden side. Fawn M. Brodie rightly emphasizes the passage in which Burton clearly expresses his scale of values:

> *Describing the natives of Abeokuta, [Burton] wrote: 'The male figure here, as all the world over, is notably superior, as amongst the lower animals, to that of the female. The latter is a system of soft, curved, and rounded lines, graceful, but meaningless and monotonous. The former excels it in variety of form and in sinew.'*

But what must have transformed her anxious concern into a state of anguish and exasperation was her husband's decision to trans-

---

[4]In his books written during his stay later on in Fernando Po, he repeats his insulting generalizations concerning blacks and makes even more reprehensible ones, full of obvious contempt and animosity. His problems with alcoholism and the ambivalence of his relations with Isabel partially explain his exaggerated, negative vision, though they do not excuse it. The only blacks who earn his sympathy and respect are, most significantly, Moslems. According to Burton, Christianity contributes to the degradation of blacks, and with great perspicacity he prophesies that sooner or later Africans will find in Islam "their natural religion."

[5]Had he known of it, Burton would no doubt have translated with enthusiasm Ahmad Al Tifachi's *The Heart's Delights*, a work that has recently appeared in French. In it the author, among many other practical pieces of advice, lays down the rules for a gentle and painless anal penetration, recommends unguents and postures, describes the attributes of a good male member, etc., not forgetting to sing the praises, at every turn, of the wisdom of the Merciful and Compassionate One.

late the classics of erotic literature, and his increasingly close association with professional erotologists such as Lord Houghton, Richard Monckton Milnes, Fred Hankey, Frank Harris, and Henry Spenser Ashbee. The physical and intellectual spell seductively cast by Burton over Swinburne—whose effeminacy, masochism, and dipsomania could not have passed unnoticed by anyone—, their frequent drinking bouts together, and—something that truly was a secret, divulged only by the poet in his letters—the violence and acts of brutality on the part of the captain, who is "too strong," Swinburne confesses, for his tastes and needs, would surely have provoked Isabel's sense of holy horror if she had had any knowledge either of the intimacy that existed between the two men or of her husband's cruel impulses and his interest in flagellation.[6] Though the unexpurgated version of *The Thousand Nights and One Night* was enthusiastically received both by the public and by the critics, it could not fail to offend Isabel's prudishness: she pretended to the outside world that she had never read it, but the truth of the matter is that those copies of it belonging to her, today the property of the Royal Anthropological Institute, were full of lines blotted out, erasures, changes, and commentaries in her own hand, a job of censorship worthy of our most upright functionaries in the Spanish Ministry of Information and Tourism in the days of Arias Salgado. On practically the eve of his death, she wrung from her husband the promise never to write on the subject again. His passing on was no doubt a relief to her: Richard could now enter the ideal kingdom of her fantasies, as he had done before their marriage, and thenceforth she could live with him her great love and reconstruct his life story without running into stumbling blocks or conflicting versions.

Burton's intimate journals probably did not contain a "minutely detailed self-portrait from the waist down" resembling the one to be found in *My Secret Life,* a work recently attributed to "Pisanus Fraxi"—the pseudonym used by the tireless lecher H. S. Ashbee, Burton's friend and mentor—whose integrity and strength of character Jaime Gil de Biedma rightly emphasizes.[7] Nonetheless, it is tempting to think that the journals might have contained such a portrait, and the friendship that united the two

---

[6]Burton mentions with obvious fascination the custom among Somali bridegrooms of whipping their brides severely on the wedding night. On the relation between Burton and the poet, see *The Swinburne Letters* (Yale University Press, New Haven: 1959).

[7]*El pie de la letra* (Barcelona: 1980).

men would make such a conjecture plausible: the hatred of Victorian society so splendidly portrayed by Steven Marcus was equally strong in both of them, and their common rehabilitation of the so-called "base" impulses had manifestly moral overtones in both. The "madness" that Isabel noted in her husband was that of a man stifling to death from the hypocrisy round about him and seeking within other cultures a freedom and a tolerance that were non-existent in his own. The portrait that Wilfred Blunt paints of him in middle age shows a Burton whose look of a "released convict," with "a countenance the most sinister I have ever seen, dark, cruel, treacherous," and "with eyes like a wild beast's" reminds him of "a black leopard, caged, but unforgiving." His perpetual exile was as much an escape from the English life he found unbearable as from the Mr. Hyde crouching within himself. To speak of the vice against nature, he would say, is sheer nonsense: what constitutes part of nature cannot be against it. Much wiser and more understanding, the Arabs preach by example that *naturalia non sunt turpa* and *mundis omnia munda*. With all its rags and tatters and miseries, for the Victorian artist and intellectual the Orient was the promise of Liberation.

The extensive and scholarly commentary on homosexuality that appears in the "Terminal Essay" of *The Thousand Nights and One Night* is, as we realize today, a daring precursor of the sexology founded by Havelock Ellis and popularized half a century later by the Kinsey Report. To speak of the "abominable vice"— "Vice" with a capital letter—, he adopts an expository, medical, "scientific" tone that, without justifying it openly, nonetheless avoids any sort of moral condemnation of it. This was something entirely new in the England that regarded every "unnatural" sex act between consenting adults as a crime and duly punished those found guilty of having committed it, sending Oscar Wilde himself to prison for it years later. The presumed objectivity of Burton's opinion on the subject fortunately did not exclude reference to facts that he had gathered first hand: the itch to know excused an incursion into forbidden territory, and Flaubert himself, we must not forget, had decided to educate himself "at government expense" by trying "this method of ejaculation" in Egypt. But unlike Burton—whom his colleague and rival Captain J. H. Speke, not content with robbing him of the laurels of having discovered Lake Victoria, and resentful perhaps of having had to yield his place in the bed of his comrade to native girls, enviously accused of being a practicing homosexual—, the French novelist had halted on the threshold of the actual test, being possibly acquainted with the anecdote attributed to Voltaire, according to which the latter, having agreed to have a try at the "execrable act" with a young and handsome English cavalier without either of them obtaining the slightest satisfaction from it, later received a letter from the Britisher in which he passed on to him the news that he had tried it again, whereupon the author of *Candide* is reputed to have remarked: "Once, a philosopher; twice, a bugger."

Burton endeavors to trace a history of homosexuality, whose origin goes back, as he writes with disarming simplicity, "to the night of time." Once the reader has gotten past Burton's tedious accumulation of rather inaccurate data on Greek and Roman homosexuals, drawn in large part from the work of his friend Ashbee, what shows through very clearly is the typical self-justifying argument that attempts to prove that from Alexander to Napoleon, from Shakespeare to Peter the Great, all men of genius were *ex illis*—ones of that particular persuasion—, an attitude that Proust eloquently denounced in his masterful portrait of Charlus. Moreover, though he was not yet acquainted with the works of Ubrichs and Krafft-Ebing on the subject, the reading of which was later urged on him by J. A. Symonds, he leaned heavily upon the picturesque medico-legal studies of Dr. Tardieu to draw up a sort of guidebook, which today we would call a "gay guide" of European capitals, indicating the best districts for "cruising" and other such piquant details. As is common knowledge, Dr. Tardieu's studies provided the writers of the first edition of the *Grande Encyclopédie Larousse* the materials for its long and marvelously funny entry on pederasty: a tissue of anecdotes, both horrifying and fascinating, about celebrated transvestites of the period for instance, one of whom, known as the Queen of England, strolled through the parks doing crochet work, or about ill-starred notables of the world of high society whose fateful passion led them, o horror of horrors, to lavish kisses upon the bare feet of little boys. In my youth, reading this article, along with the epigraph devoted to masturbation—for which, we read, matrimony is a "heroic remedy"—, was one of the most enjoyable and constructive ways of spending time during summer vacations.

What is of more interest to us are Burton's debatable, and indeed downright odd theories according to which homosexuality, far from being a physiological disorder or a perverse vice, has its source, first and foremost, in geographical and climatic factors. In his opinion, there exists what he calls a Sotadic Zone—named after Sotades, the Greek poet—, which encompasses the shores of the Mediterranean, North Africa, the Near East, Persia, Afghanistan, part of the Indian subcontinent, etc., in which "the Vice" is supposedly popular and endemic, and regarded even in the very worst of cases as a mere peccadillo. In this zone, a mixture of masculine and feminine temperaments takes place, he claims, thus explaining the widespread dissemination of both pederasty and tribadism. Though Burton emphasizes the Koranic condemnation of the sin of Lot, he also points out that throughout history, Islam has shown greater indulgence toward it than Christianity. The Moors, he says—apparently without even noticing the scarcely credible nature of his hasty generalizations—are notorious sodomites, and from Morocco the custom has spread throughout Algeria, Tunisia, and Tripoli, finally reaching Egypt, "that classical region of all abominations"; from there, the Sotadic Zone has spread to embrace Asia Minor and Mesopotamia: "the 'unspeakable Turk' " is "a race of born pederasts," and both the Druses and the Syrians follow Turkish example. Though the Bedouins know nothing of the existence of sodomy, Yemen, on the other hand, is "thoroughly infected." In Persia—in Burton's time as in the days of Chardin—houses of male prostitution abound, in which the youngsters are readied with consummate care, by way of a special diet, baths, depilation, unguents, and a series of cosmetic tricks. The Afghans, in turn, travel about accompanied by young boys and adolescents dressed as women, with their eyes painted with *kohl*, their hair in braids, their cheeks rouged, and their feet and hands dyed with henna: they are known as "wandering wives" whose "husbands" seat them in luxurious saddles on the backs of camels and walk patiently at their sides. It is true, as the refrain has it:

> The worth of the slit the Afghan knows
> The worth of the hole, the Kabul man . . .

Though Burton seasons his exposition with curious, amusing, and sometimes salacious little stories that reflect an obsessive preoccupation with the subject along with the incredible variety and wealth of his knowledge, he carefully avoids personal confession. The perpetual civil war with himself and his increasing dependence on Isabel as he approaches old age, deprive literature of an emulator of Pepys, Rousseau, or the admirable Jules Michelet, whose *Journal* describes with delectation his maniacal pleasure on sniffing his wife's undergarments after she has menstruated: a magnificent lesson in complete frankness for our timid, amnesiac, ridiculous authors of memoirs![8]

---

[8]The only work of the same sort that I know of is that of Caro Baroja. The truth of the matter is that, in the cultural desert of today's Spain, with its pretentious nobodies of both the old and the new schools, he is one of the rare writers who do not carefully edit out of their books every last trace of originality and talent.

I am not blind to the fact that individual liberation in the Middle East and in North Africa, that sentimental, sexual, and moral education through travel, as exemplified by authors as different as Gide, Tony Duvert, or Pierre Guyotat, can be viewed, from a Third World perspective, as simply one more manifestation of the colonizer-colonized dialectic, in which the Occidental, as I have written elsewhere, not only possesses or enjoys the alien body, but also analyzes it, interprets it, speaks for it, assumes its voice. The intimate self-realization of the European does not free the "native" man or woman of his or her iniquitous, horrible conditions of economic and cultural inferiority. But the personal factor plays a decisive role; there is no comparison possible between, for example, the cynical and hedonistic attitude of Flaubert and that of a Jean Genet who transmutes the inner impulse into a manner of intuiting and revealing an alien oppression, which up until that point has never found literary expression. The alchemy through which passion is transmuted by a body—a physical and cultural model of a body—into a voracious form of knowledge, capable of turning the lover into a linguist, a researcher, a scholar, a poet; of making him leap from the individual to the collective and opening his eyes to history and its tragedies and injustices; of impelling him to join the ranks of those fighting colonialism and immerse himself in the language, literature, and thought that the beloved body evokes and represents—all of this, no matter what hypocrites and idiots may say, and by that I am referring less to the noblest part of Burton's work than to the generative nucleus of my most recent essays and novels—is a *baraka* or grace that accompanies anyone who, with incorruptible rigor and sincerity, remains faithful to what is most secret and precious within himself, and by that very fact, to the degree to which he intellectualizes and moralizes his sexual life and corporealizes his morality and his thought, metamorphoses, as André Malraux has written, our age-old destiny into consciousness.

Why I Have Chosen to Live in Paris

Some years ago, a London newspaper asked Jean Genet for an article revealing his true thoughts about England. In it Genet wrote frankly of the intolerable boredom of life in that country, the dullness of its cuisine, the mediocrity of its present-day literature, the lack of sexual attractiveness of its young people, and the unregal appearance and shopgirl tastes of its queen. After the person to whom the article was given to translate had done so, he remarked to Genet that in his opinion the latter had failed completely to grasp the traits and virtues that were responsible for the greatness of the English people. "With the Empire or without it, we are a civic-minded, disciplined people. Whereas the Italians, for instance, systematically cheat the tax collector, we take pride in religiously declaring our great wealth and income." Genet thereupon included the translator's comment in his piece and added: "England is a great country because the Italians don't pay their taxes."

When a French weekly asked me recently to set forth the reasons why I had chosen to live in Paris and to explain the ties that united me to French culture, I remembered Genet's article and answered, in somewhat the same wicked vein, the series of questions put to me by the friendly, ingenuous interviewer—at first serene and self-assured, then hesitant and tense, and finally visibly shocked.

To sum up in a few words what I told her: When I came to Paris, I did so not only to escape from the Franco regime and its miserable intellectual life, but also with the hope of encountering a much more lively and open society than ours. Crossing the Pyrenees twenty-five years ago meant the possibility of freely reading Proust, Gide, Malraux, Céline, Sartre, Camus, Artaud, Bataille; seeing Genet's, Ionesco's, Beckett's theater; following at the Cinémathèque the development of the great French film tradition. Along with this vast cultural depth there was also the attraction of a climate of political freedom and the expectation of greater social equality. To make the leap from Barcelona to Paris in those days was to cease to see life in black and white and begin to open one's eyes to all its nuances and complexities. But the liberal and cosmopolitan image of herself that France projects abroad, I hastened to add, unfortunately is not the same as that perceived by a lucid observer inside that country. Under a dictatorship such as Franco's it was impossible to see clearly how a European democracy functions. The events of the Algerian war and the racism that it unleashed in the mother country revealed to me the limits, the failings, and the contradictions of an exclusively ethnocentric perspective. Since that time I have known exactly to what extent the values of its supposed ecumenicity can be relied upon. Moreover, the trials of exile confront the writer with his own truth: no one can boast of having survived them untouched and unharmed. There are authors whose ties lie uniquely and totally with their native land, for whom exile is nothing but lost time; others adapt and become integrated, more or less successfully, with their adopted country; a third group—among whom I count myself—little by little come to feel estranged both from the country they have left and from the one in which they have taken up residence. Many abandon their mother tongue and, on the banks of the Seine, write in French. In my case this proved impossible: the writer, I am persuaded, does not choose the language that will be his, but rather the language chooses him, and for the exile language becomes his true homeland. French has never been a work-tool for me, but merely a vehicle of social communication.

"Let's talk about the present," my interviewer said. "What attraction does French culture have for you? Do you identify with any particular group of writers? Does the literary life of Montparnasse and Saint-Germain-des-Près interest you?"

"To tell you the truth, despite the fact that I have a number of writer friends, I do not identify myself with any group and do my best to stay away from the intellectual ghetto of the Left Bank. I am passionately devoted to life and sacrifice it only to literature, but I flee from literary circles like a man possessed, regardless of whether they be French, Spanish, Russian, or American. In my opinion, the more involved one becomes with a literary milieu, the more difficult it is to arrive at literature. Moreover, with a very few rare exceptions, there is nothing exciting in French culture today. Poetry has failed to produce a single name of individual import since Mallarmé. The novel is still awaiting the emergence of a practitioner of the genre whose genius rivals Céline's. Theater and cinema are languishing. Essayists of the stature of Benveniste, Barthes, Foucault, of Lévi-Strauss, are disappearing from the scene without being replaced. In general terms, I might say to the French what Sarmiento said to Spaniards a century and a half ago: 'You on this side of the Atlantic and we on ours are simply translating what comes from outside. . . .'"

"Well, even though you choose to remain on the sidelines of literary life, what authors do you read or keep company with?"

"My reading these days is oriented toward the classics or my friends' writings. One of the advantages of Paris is that, without being obliged to travel elsewhere, you have every chance of meeting on the street, or of arranging to meet in a café if you so desire, García Márquez the Colombian, Roa Bastos the Paraguayan, Carlos Fuentes the Mexican, Sarduy the Cuban, Susan Sontag the American, Calvino the Italian, Kundera the Czech, Kateb Yasin the Algerian, Semprun and Arrabal the Spaniards, Ben Yelún and Edmond El Maleh the Moroccans, Kedim Gürsel the Turk. . . ."

"Well then, what is there about the city that charms you?" my interviewer said, trying to conceal her disillusionment. "The beauty of its monuments, its cultural tradition, its way of life, the Parisian atmosphere?"

"Let's leave the atmosphere and the monuments to the tourists and the students with scholarships to the Alliance Française. What attracts me most is something seldom talked about: the immeasurable good fortune that has befallen Paris by becoming a multiracial, or better put, a mestizo medina. I believe in the virture of the dynamic, fruitful mingling of cultures and ethnic groups: the New York model of the melting pot. I myself live, for instance, in Le Sentier, a section of Paris enlivened by the presence of émigrés from some twenty countries: Jewish tradesmen and *pieds noirs*, people of French origin from the former colonies, live side by side there with Spaniards, Portuguese, Turks, Algerians, Yugoslavs, Pakistanis, Moroccans, Vietnamese, Martiniquais. At certain hours of the day it is a veritable Babel of languages. The streetside walls of buildings are covered with drawings and graffiti in Arabic that native Parisians do not understand and that I decipher with genuine delight. Slowly, insidiously, Paris is becoming *third-worldized;* the emigrants and their families bring with them their customs, dress, hairdos, music, adornments, culinary habits. The modest quarters of the city are becoming much gayer and more colorful: the Parisians who live there have the marvelous opportunity—I would say the undeserved honor—of coming into contact with men, women, and children who come from very different horizons, of learning to respect each other's differences, of rubbing elbows with them at work, in cafés, or at school. Suddenly, the petty, tedious ethnocentric vision of things dissolves; accepted values come to be seen as relative, not absolute ones; prejudices and fears lose their importance. The monumental papier-mâché Paris—the Arc de Triomphe and the Tomb of the Unknown Soldier—still exists for the grande bourgeoisie, for government dignitaries, for oldsters with independent means living on their retirement incomes, for war widows. In the other Paris—the real, living Paris—*hammams* and cheap couscous restaurants proliferate like mushrooms. African drums, Berber rebecs, Indoamerican musical instruments echo in the corridors of the Métro. With every passing day, the street vendors' displays of totems and elephant tusks take up a bit more space on the sidewalks. The packing cases on which bets are laid down in games of chance as bait to lure the sucker standing around watching have all at once been translated from Xemáa el Fná to Barbès to the Grands Boulevards: today they attract a swarm of curious onlookers just a few yards from the theater where Coluche, the comedian who is a candidate for the presidency, is performing, and with a little luck we will soon see him installed in the presidential palace on the Champs-Élysées.''

"If I understand you rightly, French cosmopolitanism . . . ''

"There is no such thing as French cosmopolitanism; there is interculturalism, plurality, osmosis: a universe in miniature. If a person so desires, he can eat in a Cambodian restaurant, drink mint tea in a Moorish café, see a Hindu or a Turkish movie in the afternoon—Yilmaz Güney's *The Sheepflock* in my opinion is one of the best films of the year—and in the evening, with a bit of luck, attend a concert of the Noss el Ghiwán or Izanzaren. Society is linked to the idea of space, but culture—like the individual—is mobile, drifting like the wind. Culture today cannot be French or Spanish, or even European, but rather mestizo, bastard, fecundated by the civilizations that have been victims of our self-castrating, aberrant ethnocentricism. For if up until now we have exported the Occidental model with all its props—from its ideology to its drugs and gadgets—we are at present witnessing an inverse process that personally fascinates and delights me: the gradual dissolution of "white" culture by all the peoples who, having been forcibly subjected to it, have assimilated the tricks, the techniques necessary to contaminate it.

"So then, Paris for you. . . ''

"Insofar as it abandons its pretensions of being a beacon and accepts its status as a motley, bastard, heterogeneous metropolis that belongs to no country, I will always feel better in it than in any other exclusively 'national' city that is uniform, chaste, compact, rid of its angels.''

La Chanca, Twenty Years After

If every man has a value identical to that of every other, any corner of the world, even the most primitive and wretched, merits the same interest and recognition we ordinarily accord our own, a poet whom I quote from memory has written. This statement, if true, would serve to explain on the one hand my indifference to the country or rather the countries in which, through a series of historical accidents, the greater part of my life has been spent, and on the other hand the emotion—feelings of closeness, familiarity, warm sympathy—that very often overcomes me when I encounter disinherited peoples and regions.

My visit to Almería in 1956 was a crucial one in this respect, and to say that its influence on my future personal, esthetic, and political choices was a profound one is not at all an exaggeration: the attraction I felt for its landscapes and its people has marked me forever; when, because I went into exile, I ceased to explore the countryside of Níjar and the cruel but fascinating world of La Chanca, I found it only natural to seek to prolong in the lands and with the peoples of North Africa the relationship that I had established with Almería. Despite my Basque background and my birth in Catalonia, I have never identified with what is Basque or Catalan; nor, despite my many years' residence in France, have I ever sought assimilation with what is French. The secret affinities I have discovered are always with men and regions that are foreign and even alien to me: a reaching-out perhaps doomed to failure in view of the distance that separates the individual described on my passport and the ungraspable object of my identification.

My wandering through La Chanca and the Sierra de Gata brought me face to face for the first time with the cruel constellation of problems confronting the Third World: underdevelopment, illiteracy, injustice, resignation, institutionalized violence. Twenty-some years ago, Almería was not a Spanish province that resembled the ones with which I was familiar. For century upon century, the policy of neglect on the part of successive regimes had ruined its original sources of wealth and reduced it to the status of a wretched colony: the Almerian oppressed in his home territory, his *patria chica,* emigrated and was exploited still in the industrial regions of the North. Yet at the same time that I was making this painful discovery, the contemplation of its gorgeous, luminous countryside left me awestruck. From that time on, I have been caught on the horns of an insoluble dilemma: trapped between the esthetic and hedonistic vision of the world on the one hand, and on the other a concern that is exclusively moral. My indignation in the face of the poverty and destitution in which the men and women to whom I feel closest live enters into violent conflict with the intimate attraction I feel for a harsh, bare landscape, for a set of strong native virtues being inexorably swept away by progress and industrialization. To allow myself to be guided only by the first consideration would be tantamount to writing pamphlets denouncing the social order; to abandon myself unreservedly to the second would amount to a grave betrayal of human solidarity and sympathy. This bloodless civil war admits of no peace treaties or truces: over the years the clash of opposing principles and emotions has become a basic personality trait of mine.

Volvemos al lugar como el culpable/ retorna siempre al sitio de su crimen:[1] to journey to Almería is to go back to a turning point in my life, a baptism, beset with doubts and questions as to the validity of my earlier accounts. Ought we to conclude, with Gaston Bachelard, that scientific objectivity is not possible if we have been unable to resist the spell of the original image, if we have not carefully weighed in the balance the thoughts that leapt to mind at the time of our initial observation? Without attempting here to refute him, I shall merely say in passing that there is an irreplaceable truth inherent in our initial vision of things. The outsider apprehends a scene with a force unblunted by familiarity, with a clarity undimmed by his later probings. Recreating this initial virginity constitutes, as the formalists clearly saw, one of the fundamental purposes of the work of art: brushing away from our eyes the spiderwebs of habit, though later our perceptive exuberance must be tempered with a rigorous, and if possible exhaustive, analysis of the object of our contemplation.

The impact, however, of the traveler, the curious bystander, or the witness gives rise to questions with even broader implications. Isn't the act of describing a group to which one does not belong—even if that act is motivated by warm human sympathy and a sense of solidarity—a form of violating its privacy, of turning it into a subject for public debate and discussion, of converting it into an object on exhibition? The men and women who have been portrayed in the prose of the outsider may think so. Is there not an egocentric tendency on the part of the writer that leads him to conclude that his own standards and criteria are universal? The answer to these questions is doubtless yes, and thus the outsider is

---

[1] *Let us go back to the place as the guilty party/ always returns to the scene of the crime. (Translator's Note.)*

obliged to proceed with caution. Whatever cultural milieu the writer belongs to, he will never be neutral or innocent: the moment he undertakes to describe a world different from his own, his work will bear the indelible imprint of his own background. On setting before his readers the literary image of the vital ambiance and the mode of life of others, the outsider is duty-bound to include within it his own situation, his own way of life, his own social praxis. Once this requisite is met—and at the risk of appearing to put forth a self-serving argument by so stating—, I shall venture to say that an outsider's view of us fulfills an important function, as important as the gaze of our neighbor in shaping us and providing us with an essential part of our knowledge of ourselves. With all due reservations regarding the subjective viewpoint, the curiosity, sympathy, and interest that give rise to the personal account deserve to be defended against those who, out of a punctilious and prideful sense of reserve, challenge its legitimacy.

Since the days when I ceased to visit Almería, a good deal of water has gone under the bridge, even in a region where rain capriciously forgets to fall. A physical distancing on my part, though not an emotional one. Its painfully acute problems led to a series of reflections on underdevelopment in Andalusia, unfortunately still as timely as when I included them in an essay entitled "Tierras del Sur"—Lands of the South. Its image, "poor still, and profaned, drained and divided, centuries old and still an orphan," reappears obsessively in my novel *Marks of Identity*. Once its traditional resources had been plundered one by one, the mob of speculators in its sunshine (its last free, violent, incandescent gift of nature) and its attractions for the film industry (its unexpected calling as a latter-day Hollywood) slowly transformed its way of life, gradually bettered the lot of its inhabitants somewhat. Its landscape often appeared in movies—a living reality for me, quite apart from the plot (almost always completely inane) of the film shown on the screen. One time it was the little rectangular white hovels of Hornichuelas and the deserted beaches of La Isleta and Las Negras in a Beatles movie; another time the steep slope that leads to the top of La Alcazaba and its impressive lookout point, evocatively captured by Antonioni's camera. Usually its rugged terrain, so picturesque to the eyes of the outsider and so forbidding to the eyes of those born there, served as the background for one of those pseudo-Mexican westerns popularized by Sergio Leone, and my memory tried to locate and give a name to each scene in the background, screening out the action-packed plot and the heroic exploits of the actors in the foreground. I remember that one day, during a faculty meeting at New York Uni-

41

versity, a rather snobbish Yankee colleague of mine began chatting about Spain with her neighbors and announced that she had just purchased a "marvelous cave" in La Chanca that she was "doing over." Her words, I confess, came as a blow to me, and I was obliged to conceal my feelings. My memories of the place, so cruel and intense, were almost impossible to reconcile with the thought of a real estate investment by tourists hungry for local color. Once over my initial shock, I was ashamed of my moral indignation and concluded, perhaps naively, that the economic take-off of the '70s had radically changed that miserable suburban slum and brought a certain measure of well-being to its inhabitants.

On returning to Almería, I am assailed by doubts. Níjar, La Chanca, Rodalquilar, Carboneras, Garrucha—all the places that I would describe as close to my heart if that expression had not been worn thin to the point of meaninglessness *ad vitam æternam* by Franco's penny-a-liners—have changed for the better, but the causes of the age-old social injustice in Andalusia have not yet been remedied. Lack of capital, unemployment, the bloodletting of mass migration, demographic imbalance, under-use of resources, and in general an economy dependent on the industrial zones of the North and the revenue brought in by foreign tourism affect Almería as they do the other provinces in the South: the income per capita in Andalusia is a third lower than the average in the remainder of the country; 19% of its active population enters the vast Spanish army of the unemployed. The only inheritance that many parents can pass on to their children is still a suitcase and a train ticket to Madrid, Catalonia, France, or Germany, in a period when the worldwide economic crisis is producing more and more drastic protectionist measures and closing all the traditional escape valves one after the other. Despite development in certain limited sectors, the socio-economic depression that I have witnessed at first hand is taking Andalusia back, if not to a Third World existence, at least to a more and more marginal one on the edges of the larger cities, with no open horizons.

The traveler returning today after a long absence does not find the same brutal contrasts that he noted before: hunger, nakedness, illiteracy, tracoma have disappeared. But an oppressive awareness of underdevelopment torments him still. He experiences mixed feelings: sadness, nostalgia, and sometimes anger in the face of stubborn Spanish iniquities, and the next moment a deepfelt happiness tinged with remorse as he furtively roams about cities and towns whose layout he knows by heart—afraid, like Homer's wandering hero on sighting Ithaca, of what awaits him at his home and fireside and of the hostile barking of the dogs.

Living in Turkey

I had been promising myself that I'd go see it, but I didn't get around to it until the very last minute, just a few hours before flight time. I had feared the worst, and as usually happens in such cases, the reality surpassed the product of my feeble imagination. The accumulation of clichés, collective fantasies, ethnocentric value judgments so brilliantly analyzed by Edward Said in his recent study entitled *Orientalism,* makes it the best paradigm of a racist movie to have come along in recent years. I am referring, of course, to *Midnight Express.*

In the Nazi era, Dr. Goebbels's propaganda services backed the famous film *Jew Süss,* which summed up and distilled to their quintessence the anti-Semitic stereotypes of a vast sector of the German population. I do not know if those responsible for *Midnight Express* made the film with the deliberate intention of creating a racial bogeyman or if they did so in all "innocence": the truth remains that the violent, almost visceral venting of their feelings toward an entire people—not a single "good" Turk ever appears on the screen—apes the dubious example of their predecessors.

An exaggeration on my part? Anyone who has seen the film will remember as readily as I do the chilling succession of derogatory statements, bald accusations, gross insults which, had they had as their target the Jewish people today, would rightly have aroused the indignant protest of the entire world (the objects of race hatred change; racism endures): the Turkish people are portrayed, in the crudest brushstrokes, as a cunning, lying, servile lot, to whom all notions of nobility, justice, and mercy are totally alien. For the criticism of *Midnight Express* is not limited to the prison universe—the Turkish one in Alan Parker's film is scarcely different from those in the rest of the world—but, on the contrary, points beyond it to an entire nation: as the scenes of violence and torture take place, popular songs or Islamic prayers are heard in the background, an effect intended to create an association of ideas in the film viewer's mind between the "essence of a people" as expressed by way of their folk culture and their religion, and the brutality that he is witnessing on the screen. From the depths of the Dantesque abyss to which his unlucky star has led him, the hapless protagonist screams out his hatred of Turkey and the Turks, and his youthful vehemence is hailed—at the showing I attended, at any rate—with belligerent applause from part of the audience. Nothing, absolutely nothing escapes the rabidly denunciatory tenor of the film: not only are the Turks cruel, sodomitical, filthy, depraved; they are dreadful cooks as well (we shall come back later to the perverted culinary tastes of the hero's father, who prefers the hamburgers at the Hilton, he says, to the "awful native swill").

With the images of *Midnight Express* still fresh in my mind, I boarded the plane for Istanbul.

On my first visit to Istanbul, some eleven years ago, what struck me most forcibly—and fascinated me, once I had recovered from my initial surprise—was its aura of prodigious animal energy: a wild, omnivorous, uncontainable vitality that overwhelms the outsider the moment he sets foot in the city; the chaotic frenzy of an anthill—swarming with ants subject to some enigmatic decree of destiny—whose like I have encountered only in another metropolis of the Third World: New York, the bastard, immigrant New York of the black and Puerto Rican ghettos that little by little are changing the color of the white city and guilelessly contaminating it.

There are many anthills in the Islamic world, but in Fez, Marrakech, and even in Cairo, a subtle atmosphere of indolence suffuses—tempers—the naked aggression of street traffic. In Istanbul, as in certain areas of New York City, it follows a logic all its own, with no constraints whatsoever. Buses, pedestrians, taxis, carts invent impossible trajectories for themselves, fight their way around and through every sort of obstacle, participate in a game played according to arcane rules, obey a secret, ever-changing code.

From the quays where boats to and from Üsküdar, the Bosporus, and the Sea of Marmara dock, tens of thousands of commuters charge off daily to take the buses by storm, invade the ferry piers crowded with passengers, tramp across the drawbridge that links the two parts of the city: a rushing, resolute army of footsoldiers, voracious consumers of sandwiches and corn on the cob, elbowing their way along, coming close to downright pushing and shoving, as in subway corridors at rush hour. Leaning on the railings with their backs to the traffic, lines of anglers and idle onlookers watch the baited lines, waiting for a fish to bite. The arriving and departing boats synchronize their maneuvers, emit plumes of thick black smoke, sound their sirens in violent rhythmic blasts, load and unload passengers haughtily indifferent to the splendor of Topkapi and the minarets of Saint Sophia.

The principal obstacle for the visitor who decides, as I did, to get about "on his own" is the lack of linguistic communication.

There exist in Turkey two clearly distinct tourist circuits: the one established by travel agencies, with its sightseeing buses, Sheraton hotels, and so on; and the one created by the wave of hippies, today an obviously waning tide. Some years back, old Istanbul, especially in this neighborhood of the Mosque of Sultan Ahmed, was a vast nest of young fugitives from the detested material wellbeing of the West: at present, either because of the economic crisis (which, on affecting the parasite-ridden social body, also affects the parasites), or because of the climate of political violence that reigns in Turkey (probably one of the worst in the world), or because of the box office success of *Midnight Express* (as a matter of fact, in the lobby of the hotel where I am staying there is a notice in English warning those tempted to consume drugs that according to the laws of the land they risk rotting *eternally in prison,* a threat much more terrifying than the *life sentence* to which the marvelous translator of the warning notice doubtless was referring, inasmuch as his version implies that punishment will continue in the dungeons of the next world), the number of "marginal-looking" outlanders has diminished considerably. Not far from the Sirkeci station I ran into two Basque youngsters making their way very cautiously along the asphalt-junglesque streets, still suffering, as they readily admitted to me, from the shock of Parker's film.

Outside the travel-agency circuit (on which it is possible to find, if not guides or hotel personnel with a perfect command of some language accessible to the foreigner, a certain number of employees capable at least of coming up with a fair approximation of English or German), the vast majority of the population (including taxi drivers, desk clerks in middle-class hotels, and waiters in the best restaurants) speaks only Turkish.

Turkish—classified according to UNESCO statistics as being in eleventh place among the languages spoken today in the world: its use extends, as a matter of fact, from Edirne to Beijing—belongs to the Uralo-Altaic group, although through the centuries it has received numerous contributions of Persian and above all Arabic origin. In 1928 Kemal Ataturk replaced the traditional Arabic characters of written Turkish with a Latin alphabet, made up of twenty-nine letters whose pronunciation is clear and simple, intended to reproduce the spoken tongue with the greatest possible fidelity. At the same time he borrowed from various European languages—French in particular—a large number of technical words, also written precisely as they are pronounced. This alphabetical revolution has made Turkish one of the most phonetic languages in the world, with minimal differences between its spoken and written form. Its adaptation of a French vocabulary—shorn of the anachronistic, elitist spelling conventions of that language—makes it immediately comprehensible to Francophones and parallels the efforts on the part of French writers of the stature of a Céline (Selin), a Queneau (Keno), or a Guyotat (Guyota) to "level" their language, to make it more "plebeian," more "anti-hierarchical." As new audiovisual methods of language teaching shake the foundations of a supposed orthography that in reality is totally heterographic and do away with the mandarinate of the present-day masters of the canon, it would not appear to be overly rash to predict that written French will necessarily undergo a process of simplification similar to that successfully carried out in Turkey by Ataturk.

On a brief stroll through the streets of Istanbul, I collected the following phonetic transcriptions: *tuvalet, omlet, konfor, fuar, proje, kalite, triko, kazak, mayo, grev, bijuteri, ampül, konfeksyon, vitrin, dekorasyon, sirkulasyon, polis ekip, manto, sosis, manikür, avokat, butik, santral, kuafür elegan.* Other terms have been transliterated from Italian, English, and even Spanish: *bira, feri-bot, banyo, tiyatro, puro* (cigar), *otopista* (a metal track for fairground bumper cars), etc. Two French writers, today almost forgotten elsewhere, but still famous in these parts for their novels with a Turkish setting, have each had a city street named after them: *Pyerloti* (Pierre Loti) and *Klod Farer* (Claude Farrère). Among the best-known nightclubs of Beyoğlu there is a *Foli Berjer.*

If one knows Arabic as well as French, the language barrier—at least when it comes to the ability to read signs on the street—is not altogether unbreachable: *aile* (family), *ticaret* (shop, commercial establishment), *mektup* (menu), *çorba* (soup), *hesap* (check, bill), *mudir* (director), *baladiye* (city hall), etc. As I discovered with the aid of a little manual in English, Turkish morphology too is quite simple: there is just one declension for nouns, involving the use of six types of suffixes, and a single conjugation for regular verbs. Syntax is also very simple—subject, object, verb—, and any foreigner with an average aptitude for languages could easily establish the basis for a fundamental interchange with the inhabitants were it not for the fact that out of fear, caution, or self-protection on meeting foreigners in these difficult times in their country, Turks, or to be more precise, people in Istanbul, are not inclined to be talkative, or even communicative, in the presence of outsiders.

In Istanbul, as in New York, the fight for survival is glaringly evident—at once a brutal fact and a great stimulus. The hard necessity of earning one's daily bread, of somehow surviving the onslaughts of a general and apparently irremediable crisis is betrayed by a bristling energy that causes every movement or gesture to take on an air of brusque determination, by an intensity that at first sight appears to be excessive. Instead of resigning himself to his fate, the Turk confronts it squarely, with a healthy impulsiveness. The universal operation of the law of the jungle obliges him to be chary of his feelings and adapt himself to a competitive and hostile environment in which he cannot allow himself a single error or weakness. Amiability, courtesy, good manners are a luxury which it is best to do without, so do without them he does. The stranger feels ignored, invisible almost. People's eyes seem to stare straight through him at some object situated behind him. This non-existence, apart from the mere basic interchange of services, nonetheless has its advantages. The visitor in turn transforms himself into a movie camera that coldly records, with unfeeling curiosity, the extraordinary microcosm that surrounds him: the endless hustle and bustle of people in the street markets; delivery boys bowed down beneath loads much too heavy for them; versatile vendors whose stock in trade includes caps, handkerchiefs, rings of pastry, lottery tickets; pushers of contraband tobacco who furtively offer the passerby a peek at a coveted pack of Marlboros. As there is little work available and the price of a whole pack of American cigarettes—fifty liras—is beyond the reach of most, ingenious hustlers sell them singly. Soldiers with fixed bayonets slyly keep an eye open for this sort of trafficking and step into the picture to confiscate the wares of any peddler imprudent enough or stupid enough not to have taken the elementary precaution of greasing their palms before doing business.

The system of organized tours—planes, sightseeing buses, guided visits, de luxe accommodations—accounts for 95% of Turkish tourism. These travel agency clients all follow the same circuits, and their only contact with the population is with the tour guides and hotel personnel. The Germans rank first, followed by the Dutch, the Americans, and—who would ever have suspected as much!—the Spanish, particularly numerous at this season. On the deck of the boat taking me to Anadolu, a group of them who have recently encased themselves in leather at the Grand Bazaar in Istanbul rant and rave against our corrupt and ominous democracy, and to judge from their nostalgia, worthy of that of defeated Confederates after the War of Secession, I deduce that under Franco's regime we had more of everything, including sun.

47

Two brief tales of chance spiritual encounters with my compatriots:

> At the entrance to the Mosque of Sultan Ahmed,
> a sign reminds non-Moslem visitors that shoes must
> be removed. A middle-aged man, with the simon-pure,
> vox-populi accent of the Madrid suburb of Chamberí:
> "Piss on that! I'm not going in then!"

> On the lower deck of the Karaköy Bridge,
> Turkish devotees of the narghile inhale with
> intense concentration the smoke that filters
> through the glass bowl filled with scented water.
> Suddenly a horrified female at my back:
> "Look, Paco! They're drug addicts!"

(Fortunately for me, I also came across the Basque youngsters, with whom I had a most pleasant conversation.)

A conspicuous absence: the French.

During the autumn I spent in Turkey, I rarely ran into French tourists, as though their spectacular decline in recent years, culturally and linguistically—in the face of American English and above all German—had dissuaded them from visiting these parts.

In 1968 there was a little daily paper in Istanbul, called *Le Journal d'Orient,* in which one could read Victor Hugo and Eugène Sue in installments. Its unusual layout made no distinction between news items, prepublication excerpts from books, the leisure section, the thoughtful burblings of one or another gassy thinker. (I one day discovered a France-Presse dispatch, backed into a corner by a horoscope, announcing the fateful news that was to oblige me to cut my visit short: the franc had been devalued.) The linotype operators, moreover, appeared to have gradually lost their grasp of the language, and the items printed were full of typographical errors ("a daily paper consisting of errors with a few texts," Borges would have said). Between my two visits, *Le Journal d'Orient* ceased to appear—having lost through old age, death, or emigration both its perpetrators and its readers.

The harmonious combination of vital energy, physical strength and, often, handsome features contrives to make the Turkish male a magnetic, unusually attractive individual. The party in question knows it and carefully cultivates his macho image with feminine coquetry. While the Anatolian peasant accepts without complexes his rough-and-ready appearance, his resemblance to a wrestler or a weight-lifter, the city-dweller, even one of modest means, tends to imitate as closely as possible an ideal model: a combination of Mark Spitz and Omar Sharif, an elegant, commanding presence. Today's urbanized Turk conforms, perhaps unwittingly, to the masculine ideal of the gay as envisioned in the U.S. His facial expressions, gestures, poses in public are a blend—at first glance seemingly spontaneous—of toughness and refinement. But his spotless attire, his meticulous haircut, his carefully tended mustache betray a secret desire to seduce: here, as in other latitudes, this inordinate, aggressively flaunted virility is a signal beamed by the male to his own sex (outside middle-class residential districts, markets, and bazaars, the Turkish woman is conspicuous by her absence. She does not veil her face as do the women in a large part of the Arab world: she is, purely and simply, an abstraction. On the Karaköy Bridge or Istiklal Caddesi the proportion of men to women is fifteen or twenty to one).

Very often, Turkish men give the impression of having stepped out of the barbershop: whether they favor the traditional hairstyle, or a short-cropped boyish cut *à la garçonne* as the younger ones do, their coiffure is impeccable, carefully calculated to attract those fetishists mesmerized by leather and revealing, skin-tight pants. But where their seductiveness manifests itself even more boldly is in their attentive cultivation of a perfectly groomed, luxuriant mustache. In any café, and even on the street, they can be seen lovingly adjusting their handlebars with the aid of a little hand mirror and then contemplating them with narcissistic satisfaction.

A Turkish mustache is always either horizontal or with the tips pointing upward: it grows out to the sides, sometimes as far as the ears, or else upward, twisted into volutes resembling an Ionic capital. A mustache with the tips pointing downward à la Pancho Villa arouses, as I have personally witnessed, reactions of hostility or stupefaction; it is the sign of an alien and vaguely threatening virility: that of the Kurd. The semiology of the Turkish mustache obeys a strict code. Stroking one's mustache as one stares one's potential adversary straight in the eye is the worst of insults: it is the equivalent of the European forearm-sawing "up yours" gesture or the American upraised middle finger. Like the language in bygone days of the wink of the eye or the fan, the foreign spectator who wishes to understand the game being played must take the time to learn its basic rules.

For years now I have been attending showings of movies meant for a North African public: a repertory consisting mainly of Arab and Hindu features and karate films. While comedies or psychological dramas from Europe or the United States are of no interest whatsoever to the Third World moviegoer, the wild plots and hair-raising episodes of these films that I have mentioned—the magic spells, abductions, bloody revenges, allegories, soliloquies, songs, talking animals—fulfill the desires and dreams of peoples highly receptive to the pleasure of what Blanco White called "incredible imaginings": it is not for nothing that the story line of popular Egyptian or Hindu movies faithfully follows that of the classic Byzantine novel.

Curiously enough, the impact of Ataturk's cultural revolution has profoundly changed the tastes and sensibilities of the Turkish public, weaning it away from the infantile and ingenuous fantasies that hold the masses of Delhi, Karachi, Cairo, Tunis, or Fez spellbound. Bruce Lee and his acolytes admittedly waken enormous enthusiasm, but the movie advertisements in the newspapers and on billboards usually tout other sorts of film productions: the inevitable American war movie and, a notable fact since this is an Islamic country, the products of the flourishing national porn industry.

To judge from the advertisements and billboards, the Turkish erotic movie has an eminently educational function: with different variations and settings, depending on the inventiveness of the illustrator, the Spitz-Sharif male lead shown in them is invariably visiting an exemplary punishment—one of those thorough beatings that in comic books give off lightning bolts or sparks—upon a scantily-clad woman (presumably of scant virtue as well), whom we sometimes see prostrated at the feet of her contemptuous chastiser, and at others, clutching his knees in a gesture of supplication.

With the exception of a very beautiful film by Yilmaz Gunçy, denouncing the feudalism and backwardness of Turkish rural areas, the half-dozen movies I saw during my stay all had the same plot line: Spitz-Sharif, the prosperous owner of a splendid villa and a white Mercedes convertible, held interminable telephone conversations, as his manservant-confidant gently massaged his back, with a Carmencita-Franco-at-the-age-of-twenty type, sometimes a brunette and sometimes a peroxide blonde, also the fortunate possessor of a villa and a convertible, and also being massaged, by a winning, compliant maidservant. The camera shifted back and forth between telephoner and telephonee and between one bed and the other, one white telephone and the other, till the moment, eagerly awaited by all, when (after a resounding slap in the face or without one) Spitz-Sharif and the pseudo-Carmencita tested the elasticity of the bedsprings and the firmness of the coilspring mattress, with a background sound track full of wild moans and cries.

The image of the brutal and bullying macho presented in films and photo-romances bears, happily, little relation to reality. Despite the tensions and difficulties of everyday life, Turks are possessed of a fair amount of warmth and cordiality that tempers the rudeness and crudeness of their manners: after a long and violent argument over the price of a taxi ride—the meter never works and the taxi drivers fix the price by sizing up what can be extorted from the passenger—the driver (cap, sleeveless jacket, green eyes, pale eyelashes) smiles, wants to know what country I'm from, asks me what I think of the city, holds out a pack of Samsuns, and when I tell him I don't smoke, pulls an atomizer out of his pocket and perfumes me with orange-flower water. In the bus on my way to Konya, a peasant couple offer to share their lunch with me: a little while later, the woman has fallen asleep with her head on her husband's shoulder, and he brushes the breadcrumbs from her skirt with infinite tenderness.

The interurban bus service is modern and efficient, and allows the visitor to travel around most of the country quickly and comfortably. The fierce competition between companies covering the same routes forces them to include in the fare—frankly cheap, even in terms of a dollar that at the time of my visit was very low—certain supplementary amenities such as music, caramels, peanuts, and after each stop, the ritual of a few drops of cologne on the passengers' hands.

In my travels through the western provinces of Anatolia I did not run into a single tourist anywhere. At one of the stops, the driver's helper—the same shaggy-haired boy who has just perfumed me—plants himself in front of my camera and asks me to take his picture. I accede to his wishes, but to my surprise he does not give me his address so that I can send him a print. When I tell this story in Istanbul, a compatriot of his enlightens me: he simply wanted his image to get around.

Turkish driving style is sometimes wild and always temperamental: with the greatest serenity in the world, they are capable of passing on a curve or a blind hill, merely (in the best of cases) giving warning of their maneuver by honking furiously. The traffic police of Istanbul majestically preside over the chaos, taking no exception to the bold moves of the fearless charioteers. No one, or almost no one, pays the least attention to the color of the traffic lights and a fair number of taxi drivers indulge, with visible satisfaction, in the delightful sport of bagging pedestrians. Nonetheless there are few accidents, and despite the many motor vehicles the flow of traffic is ordinarily miraculously smooth and free of bottlenecks. The local traffic authorities have adopted the old motto of the physiocrats: *laissez faire, laissez passer, le monde va de lui-même,* and mysteriously, the facts seem to prove them right.

The provincial capitals live a peaceful existence, the diametrical opposite of the fear and agitation that reign in Istanbul. The townspeople of Konya are friendly and hospitable, and the stranger who comes to visit the admirable Mosque of Aladdin or the museum of Islamic art where the dervishes perform their dances will have no difficulty establishing contact with local people if he is so inclined. The entire city worships the memory of the great poet and mystic Maulana Khalal Din Rumi, the creator of the extraordinary choreography through which the dervish communes with God, and the author of the celebrated verses dedicated to his friend and spiritual guide Shams Tabriz:

> *I was snow, and your rays melted me.*
> *The earth drank me in; a mist of the spirit,*
> *I rise toward the sun.*

Another particularity of Konya: the noticeably smaller number of lawyers' and drugstore signs, whose proliferation in Bursa, Istanbul, or Ankara sometimes takes on the dimensions of a real nightmare. (In a single residential block it is possible to find up to four and five pharmacies, and to judge from the *avukat* nameplates and signs attorneys occupy entire buildings around the Palace of Justice and in the office districts of the city.)

In a modest restaurant in Konya, a loquacious, nervous, slender policeman comes over, sits down at my table, and tells me, in fair French, that he has traveled all through Europe, been a restaurant waiter in Geneva, and dreams of going back to Switzerland. After a few minutes he shows me the letter he has received from an English lady tourist with whom he has had an idyllic affair, and asks me to translate it for him. The tone of the missive is conventional, but he explains to me that she loves him and is eager to see him. He was mad enough to listen to his parents and come back to his country; now he's a policeman and can no longer travel abroad as he once did. Do I know the Teksas Casino, next to the Aladdin Park? They serve alcohol there, the way they do in Istanbul, and there are women, and if I'd like to, he proposes feverishly, he'll go there with me tomorrow and have a few drinks with me, because it's his day off and he likes to spend time with foreign visitors. I answer that I won't be able to, since I'll be going on to Izmir, and he smiles sadly.

"Well, good luck then. And even though you see how poor we are, don't think badly of us," he adds with a dignified, slightly pathetic air.

It was not possible for me to sample the pleasures of the casino in Konya, with its women and its alcoholic beverages, but at a later time, back in Istanbul, I decided to go have a look inside a place next to the Sirkeci station, to the left of the little narrow street leading to my hotel. From late afternoon until well on into the night, a loudspeaker outside, doubtless designed with an audience of deaf people or holiday roisterers in Valencia in mind, broadcast the contents of its musical program to the entire neighborhood: the melodies of the songs pursued me daily, long, long after I had turned the corner and gone on down the little street with garbage cans and conclaves of cats everywhere, thanking my lucky stars that I was not one of the guests of the squalid, filthy Toros Palas Otel that I could see directly across from the cabaret, and hence was spared the auditory delights of an uninterrupted and seemingly interminable stage show. A red and green neon sign, resembling those of the many nightclubs of Beyoğlu, temptingly promises:

YENI SAZ SOLO

VARIETE — ATRAKSYON

Inside, a bare stage without backdrop or curtain, and some forty tables occupied by an exclusively male audience, with the exception of four or five middle-aged women keeping a clinical eye out for the arrival of a customer who gives signs of being drunk, timid, or a country bumpkin, so as to sit down next to him and make him pay for a drink after a few minutes of chatting him up. The waiters are serving raki and beer and bringing little plates with appetizers and slices of melon to various tables.

On the program: a folklore group made up of several adolescent boys and a girl, all of them dressed in short sleeveless jackets and balloon trousers; a sexy chanteuse—the pseudo-Carmencita?— with long peroxided locks; a blond, good-looking Spitz-Sharif with an immaculate, flashy double-breasted suit; and finally, a lively little shorty of a man who gestures a lot and clutches the microphone energetically as he sings, cradling it as though it were a baby and appearing at times to subject it to eager, almost frantic fellatio.

Once over my surprise, the most interesting spectacle is that offered by the audience: a group of happy consumers of alcohol and appetizers spurs the pint-size, passionate male singer on, with cheers and applause, to greater deeds of vocal prowess; a potbellied individual dances forward, with remarkable lightness of foot, to the stage and reaches up to tuck a handful of bills into the waistband of the girl in native costume; a tipsy young man with a limp insists on inviting customers at nearby tables over to his, finally persuades one of them to come over, and after pouring him a generous drink, covers his forehead and cheeks with fervent kisses; two men with mustaches, circles under their eyes, and somber faces, in caps and black sleeveless jackets, impassively contemplate the erotic contortions of the sexy singer as they tell the beads of their Islamic rosaries in unison (in Turkey the *sbiaa* of pious Arabs is a sort of gadget used by a great many males in the most unexpected places).

Suddenly, the performers and the audience mingle: or at any rate the diminutive singer with the suggestive, saccharine voice joins his imprudent admirers. Without breaking off his *bel canto*—the amorous tremolos appallingly amplified by the sound equipment—, the artist comes down from the stage, walks over, microphone in hand, to the nearest table, and begins to moan, to throw diva kisses, to close his eyes dreamily in front of a hefty young hick who, embarrassed by all this free publicity, withstands this lyric downpour as best he can. But the shorty continues to heave his ardent sighs, puts his hand on the rube's shoulder, brings the microphone up to his lips, as the object of this assault holds him off as best he can, lights a cigarette to keep from getting kissed, and then, cornered, all his defense tactics exhausted, abruptly rises to his feet and goes off to the toilet to urinate.

Without turning a hair, the singer comes over to me (I am the only foreigner in the place), all set to favor me with his earsplitting ballad, and in order to sidestep his move (I can all too readily picture this third-rate Turkish romeo seated on my knees, moaning his love-lyrics in my ear in a voice like a sticky caramel), I stand up, pay the check, and leave.

The *hammami* is a national institution. Obsessed, like the Arabs, with bodily cleanliness, the Turks visit the public bath regularly and spend entire evenings in it, in a pleasant, intimate, calm, relaxed atmosphere. While the Moorish bath imposes an almost religious silence—the customers abandon themselves to the ministrations of the masseur with a feminine passivity that happily compensates for their aggressive conception of virility—, the Turkish *hammami* is a social meeting-place, where the bathers congregate to talk together, with a minimum of clothes, as casually as in a café or the marketplace. With the exception of a few establishments frequented by gays—among them the old Çukurcum, which certain evil tongues call the Suck-or-Come—the baths that I am familiar with present a picture of lively social interchange and general hubbub that would be inconceivable in the world of Islam farther to the west.

The best of them, from the architectonic point of view, is the one at Yenaplika, at the entrance to Bursa, built four centuries ago by Rustem Pasha. Its immense entry hall has a magnificent green and pink mosaic floor; its main room is octagonal and opens onto eight rooms with turquoise tiled walls; the great marble pool into which the hot water is piped has marble columns at its four corners supporting the splendid cupola through which the light filters down.

When I enter, the pool is a fishpond teeming with children and adults ducking, pushing, shoving, splashing, spattering each other. I take refuge from the deafening noise in one of the steam rooms off to the side equipped with hot and cold water faucets and am absorbed in sweating and washing myself down with buckets of water when the rather odd behavior of the man next to me attracts my attention. He is an obese, bald-headed individual who, after having unknotted the towel that he has modestly girded round his privates, appears to be urinating, in utter serenity of spirit, with his face to the wall. A moment or so later, an adolescent walks over next to him, and without the slightest circumspection frankly spies on the man's movements just above his protective towel as he stands there a few inches from the wall. But the bald-headed man's presumed micturition tends to go on indefinitely, and the movements of his free, but hidden, hand (he is holding the towel round himself as best he can with the other one) now point to a more daring hypothesis. Can it be possible? I ask myself, and the unhealthy interest of the young lad, indiscreetly absorbed in the contemplation of the secret, lends further corroboration to my bold interpretation. Suddenly the presumed masturbator knots the towel around himself again, steps back, and abandons his place, whereupon I spy in the wall, some three feet up from the floor, a round hole out of which vapor is steadily pouring. It is the adolescent's turn, but he appears to have sensed my skepticism regarding the thaumaturgic powers of the hole and firmly insists that I try it. *Çok iyi, çok iyi* (very good, very good), he says, and as he sees that I am still disinclined, he adds with a persuasive smile: *gud, very gud.* Wary (though a bit curious), I move over to the wall of delectations and like my predecessor unknot my towel so that the vapor will strike my member directly.

55

The feeling is not unpleasant, but I expectantly await something more: the ineffable beatitude of the mystic, a brief though exquisite erection perhaps. Several minutes go by, and alas, nothing happens (except for a slight tickling sensation). Disappointed, I cover up my flaccid, culpable penis, and since the boy is anxiously awaiting some complimentary remark on my part, I murmur, so as not to disillusion him, an *iyi* of feeble conviction.

A few street images that I did not contrive to capture with the lens of my Pentax.

On the sidewalk invaded by stands and stalls with all manner of goods on display, a little cart full of brassieres. The vendor recites the price in a monotonous voice and two mustachioed giants, beetlebrowed and grave-faced, straight out of one of Chaplin's silent films, attentively inspect the merchandise, carefully unfold several brassieres to establish comparisons, calculate with the practiced eye of a cooper the thoracic diameters of their spouses and finally choose—or rather, one of them chooses—the biggest size, befitting the opulence of an extremely generous, plethoric, hyperdeveloped pair of breasts. The scene takes place in silence, without a trace of humor or a smile, and the pair of them melt into the crowd, visibly satisfied with the purchase.

In the neighborhood of the Grand Bazaar, baskets and tables full of cassettes, socks, caps, belts, women's apparel, sandwiches, ring-shaped pastries, corn on the cob. The delivery boys try to breast the heavy tide of buyers and a truck hemmed in by pedestrians and unable to move vainly seeks a hole in the traffic so as to inch forward. One would swear that there is not a hair's breadth of empty space left there, but the powers of the runaway Turkish imagination immediately belie this conclusion: from a narrow street jammed with people there comes rolling out, in an abrupt defiance of logic and the limits of corporeal contraction, a military tank of U.S. manufacture and its Yankee crew.

A display of porno magazines, with naked women photographed in their bed or bath, keeps a ring of spectators riveted in lustful contemplation of the disturbing, coveted female body. Meanwhile a slender, fine-boned girl, infinitely more beautiful than the admired models, passes by, hips gracefully swaying, directly alongside them without attracting the slightest attention.

A number of years ago, newsstands and bookstores in Athens offered for sale, in several languages, a book pompously entitled *The Secret of Greek Cuisine.* I remember that after enduring for a week the immutable menu of the Plaka tourist restaurants I reached the conclusion that this was the best-kept secret in the world: in any event, no Greek would appear to be in on it.

This generalization, which like all generalizations nonetheless has a certain truth to it, could in no case be applied to Turkish cuisine, of which Greek cooking—the Hellenes may say what they will—is merely a degenerated appendix.

Turkish culinary art cannot compete in refinement with the French, or within the Islamic world, with the Moroccan, but on the whole it is varied and satisfactory. If they were to sample them, my friends who are gastronomes would doubtless appreciate the delicious *mezeler* (assorted appetizers) of the very modest Konyali restaurant, the grilled fish served in the outdoor cafés on the shores of the Bosporus, the *döner kebap* (thin slices of meat grilled in a single compact block), the succulent *dolmas* (stuffed grape leaves, peppers, or mussels), et cetera. Instead of resigning himself to the tasteless hamburgers at the Hilton, the distinguished paterfamilias of *Midnight Express* might have consoled himself in the sober décor of blue-green mosaic tiles of Pandeli for the misfortunes that had befallen his offspring; there, for a very reasonable price (less than ten dollars per person), it is possible to consume *bulgare pilavi* (seasoned cracked wheat), *börek* (a sort of quiche), or *begendi kebap* (meat with eggplant sauce)—the best in Istanbul.

The waiters merit a separate paragraph. Unlike those in restaurants in the U.S.S.R., where the customer may sometimes wait half an hour before they deign to present him with the menu, the ones in Turkey have precisely the opposite failing: they serve meals at breakneck speed and obsessively snatch your plate away before you've finished eating. As a general rule, they are somewhat brusque and their lack of knowledge of any other language besides their own rather complicates the task of selecting from the menu.

In one of the restaurants near Taksim Meydani where I often went, the waiter—a very good-looking young man belonging to the Spitz-Sharif lineage—regularly awaited my order with an impenetrable look of stone on his face, without a single polite, friendly word for my painful but commendable efforts to improve my command of his language.

Finally I can bear it no longer, consult my dictionary, and suddenly transfix him:

"Why are you always so solemn?"

The young man seems to be utterly disconcerted, and does not react immediately; then little by little his features unfreeze and, still somewhat stunned, he answers my question.

As far as I can deduce from his reply, he lives by himself, far from his family, and after a few sentences that unfortunately I do not understand, he says that things are going very badly, there are people killed every day, nobody knows where the country is heading, people are afraid.

Cordiality is difficult in such circumstances, and when I come back the next time, he observes me with the usual inscrutable expression on his face, and outside the discussion of the menu, we do not exchange a single word.

The day of my departure.

At a little newsstand, the daily papers on display feature a whole new series of corpses riddled with bullets, mangled bodies, destroyed buildings, arms seized from terrorists. The passersby snatch them from the hands of the vendor, stop to leaf through them, gather in grim-faced little groups to discuss in half-whispers what has happened.

Except for one tall man, with the look of a modest office employee, who takes a sidelong glance at the horrifying spread of photos of dead bodies, spits on the ground in rage, and strides quickly on.

Ethnocentric ghosts, centuries old, cloud the Westerner's vision of the Islamic world, even of the modernized, secular link in the chain represented by today's strife-rent, unstable, contradictory, but amazingly lively post-Kemal Turkey. As Parker's despicable film proves, the country is not even viewed with the indulgence, the interest in the picturesque, or the fascination ordinarily aroused by other civilizations—Buddhism or Brahmanism, for example—because of its total otherness and remoteness: it is too near at hand to us to be exotic and too unyielding and impermeable for us to be able to tame it or to get really inside it. Felt to be closed in upon itself and unassimilable, it thus emerges, from our present hysterical perspective of a world in which "Atlantic" power is tottering and its values foundering, as a disturbing mirror that our blinders transform into a grotesque, threatening bogeyman.

Berliner Chronik

To the outsider, even a brief stay in Berlin is above all an invitation to engage in fruitful reflection on space. Razed by the war, divided in two by the irregular and obsessive trace of an absurd wall, the former capital of the Reich and of the more modest and interesting Weimar Republic has lost its center of gravity and, in the western sector at least, offers that outsider's eye a vista of vacant lots, woods, surfaces overgrown with weeds and brush, empty, deserted areas: a bizarre ecological paradise. From the elevated train crossing Kreuzberg—crowded with punks with coxcombs or hedgehog hairdos and manifestly prolific Turkish immigrants—the reader of Alfred Döblin, Walter Benjamin, or the young Nabokov discovers to his amazement that meadowlands and open country have emerged in areas once densely populated and full of life and activity. The memorable hustle and bustle and effervescence of the Anhelter Bahnhof seem to have vanished like a mirage: vegetation has covered the railroad tracks, the immense lobby and the train platforms have become sand pits, and the nearby river port is now a garden. Like Pompeii or Palmyra, the Tiergarten and Potsdamerplatz districts in the center of town are insidiously turning us into archaeologists and scholars. But its ruins do not go back two millennia: however unlikely it may seem, they are not even half a century old.

To arm ourselves with a map of the old Berlin, take the open-air elevator up to the lookout tower built next to an atomic bomb shelter, and from there—in a Rockers' bar where beer and hashish are consumed together in prodigal quantities—survey the panoramic view that takes in the gray line of the wall and the two halves of the devastated city is not only a direct invitation to mental breakdown and schizophrenia: it is a motley, dreamlike spectacle that epitomizes, without the need for hallucinogens, the prodigious historical unreality in which we live. We will search in vain for the buildings and monuments that figure on the grid squares of the map: the Air Ministry; the Gestapo Headquarters; the hotels and residential blocks around the station. We will find only expanses of grass and sand, the face of a ruined, blackened colonnade, lots full of parked trucks, trailers, and jalopies, plots of ground used to train novice drivers, buildings left miraculously unharmed and today occupied by communes, and beyond the wall that will not heal and the motionless nightmare of its searchlights, lookout posts, and mine fields, new neutralized spaces and monotonous cubes of glass and cement that, to the left of Unter den

Linden, follow one upon the other in the direction of the Alexanderplatz.

The war and the postwar period have cleared out the teeming mass of street people that once inspired wonderful Berlin chronicles: the fecund chaos of their gestures, their endless turmoil, their pitiless struggle for life. The street as described by Döblin and Isherwood was not only their refuge and vital element, but also, as in every city not "cleaned up" by the boss-state or by a sudden, gigantic hecatomb, that "womb of life in creation and movement" from which, as Élie Faure astutely observed, spirituality and artistic and literary invention always spring. On top of this intricate, imbricated, precarious, expressive space there lies today another one, vast and uninhabited, left to become a lonely wasteland: ruins, rubble, excavations that lay bare the swampy land on which the city was built. The well-known slogan of Paris students in May of '68, "Down with paving stones—a beach instead," is here a reality. After a walk through the now-vanished topography traced by Benjamin, the frustrated reader returns home with fine sand all over his shoes.

Strolling along the edge of the gardens and the heavily wooded areas of the Tiergarten toward Potsdamerplatz is a notable and more or less unique experience. Time has covered the defunct official Berlin, like a drunken Noah, with a green carpet of compassion and oblivion. On the façade of the headquarters of the Spanish diplomatic mission, above the front balcony—an ideal setting for charismatic appearances and vertical salutes—, the yoke and arrows of the Falange and an ugly Francoist escutcheon are still visible, and the visitor gratefully contemplates its rows of windows, blind and gummy with sleep, its stained and pock-marked walls, symbols indifferently declining and falling amid the vegetable splendor. Following a footpath half overrun with grass—alongside useless water faucets and ridiculous drains—, the Berlin literary stage set succumbs beneath the impact of the incredible real image: the shabby Japanese Embassy and its courtyard are now used as a humble sheep farm; the solid structure of a bunker barely resists the asphyxiating embrace of a tangle of brush, ivy, and ferns; creeping vines and trees thrive on the balconies of a jungle-like Greek legation in which the only credible ambassador would be Tarzan. The work of deciphering the urban palimpsest results in a fragmented, distorted vision of reality: at times it is sheer surrealism.

I remember that years ago, in Tijuana, I had a similar impression: I had walked for hours in the rectilinear streets lined with an endless conglomeration of bars, cockfighting pits, jai alai courts, shows topless and shows bottomless, taxi-dance places, offices of

60

shyster lawyers specializing in divorces and tax evasion, amid a crowd of hustlers, prostitutes, mariachis, and bleached blondes from the high society of San Diego and Los Angeles disguised in mantillas and high combs to attend a *corrida* in which El Cordobés was fighting, when I suddenly came upon a genuine Marxist-Leninist bookstore, well-stocked with the works of Mao, Fidel, and Che. I went inside—the door was open and there was not a soul in sight—and as I was struggling to make some sense out of the layout of the place, a pink-cheeked individual suddenly appeared, as in *The Umbrellas of Cherbourg*—cheerily singing in Catalan. Seconds later, before I had had time to recover from my shock of surprise, two young *mestizas,* with long braids and melodious accents, peeked in to ask the owner of that incredible establishment "if he had any little prints of Mesopotamia." I confess that when I stepped back out into the street, I felt as dizzy as though I had drunk, on a stupid bet, an entire bottle of Chivas Regal.

I was overcome by the same feeling of *dépaysement* and unreality as I walked back to my apartment in Kreuzberg when, on going past the only intact building in a wild, rustic expanse, I heard through an open window a voice well-known to me, that of Abdelhakim Hafez, singing "Risala men taht el ma": a sentimental Egyptian ditty resounding in the heart of a central European residential district that had first been transformed into a huge vacant lot and then into a forest preserve. Such a concatenation of improbabilities and absurdities could happen only in the delirious and paradigmatic setting of a Berlin at once forever gone and tangible, prehistoric and postnuclear.

Kreuzberg is in point of fact a microcosm that in its own way illustrates the universal absurdity: alongside the dazzlingly lighted buildings housing the Springer press group the dividing wall zigzags past, completely covered with subversive daubings. Buildings occupied by anarchist communes—recognizable by the posters hanging from their windows, their gaudy murals, and occasional black flags with skull and crossbones—overlook the watchtowers, barbed wire fences, ditches, and *chevaux de frise* of the sanitary cordon that surrounds the eastern sector of the city. In similar fashion, a bunch of immigrant children have recreated an Anatolian décor for themselves and are piling straw on a cart in a little meadow surrounded by barricades, half a dozen yards distant from the frontier drawn as a consequence of Yalta and Potsdam. Here, signs written in Turkish warn the unwary that the oil-streaked waters of the Spree belong to the other side: anyone who ventures to swim in them runs the risk of being met with bullets fired by the guards of the "popular democracy" that rules on the opposite shore. Over there, mysterious streetcar tracks emerge as though by magic from the sand and disappear, with stunning unreality, at the foot of the wall.

The space of Berlin is a rigorous superposition of strata: the lively and the exuberant world of Frank Biberkopf—the culture broth in which it lives—remains buried beneath that razed, aseptic territory in which the dethroned capital is today encamped. The present belongs to ecologists and city planners: green belts, open spaces. The alternative-lifestyle communes and immigrant neighborhoods have cropped out on the surface like an after-effect of the cataclysm: the survivors of this catastrophe look upon them as though they were inhabitants of another planet. The chaotic, creative, feverish Berlin of the '20s would seem today to be a mere fabrication had the admirable narrative art of that era not taken upon itself the task of picturing its existence for us, and had it not, through its chronicles and novels, successfully laid claim, in the face of history and its miseries, to the ultimate victory of literature.

The Crosses of Yeste

Intact, inexorable, obdurate: exactly as I have remembered it, ever since the day eighteen years ago when I discovered it alongside the ditch at the edge of the switchback road, at the foot of an arid, burned-off clearing.

A stone cross with a simple base, whose inscription, though defaced today by a vindictive hand, can nonetheless be dimly made out:

R I P

**On this spot
five Spanish gentlemen
were murdered
by the red rabble of Yeste.
A remembrance and
a prayer for their souls.**

The traveler still has a vivid recollection of this countryside, as though his memory, through all these years, had kept it from fading by evoking, with obsessive simultaneity, a series of condensed background shots. Fields of esparto grass, patches of whitish earth, rocky ground, almond orchards, viewed once again with treacherous and implacable nostalgia, fill out spaces that have never been lost, loom up with sudden sharpness of detail, take on an unexpected tangibility. The round of seasons circles monotonously and the sun shines, as ever, with fanatical persistence: the same whitewashed farmhouses, the same harvesters shaking olives from the trees with long sticks, the same herds of sheep, the same minuscule beehives melting in the heat. When the terrain changes and the green of pines appears, the ineffable smile of someone whom the traveler mistakes for Prime Minister Adolfo Suárez and who turns out to be the popular singer Manolo Escobar beams from a shed built at the intersection of the road leading to the Fuensanta dam. The stranger looks out across the blue surface of the reservoir whose arms and bays extend to the bends in the road and can see only an ocher desolation, the regular superposition of recently bared strata with trees of varying heights on the slope opposite, like a schoolroom model for a geology lesson. The drought has brought the water down to unprecedented low levels: the valleys of the Tus and the Segura, submerged for forty-seven years, suddenly revive bitter memories and inadvertently exhume episodes and stories brought to mind, a few kilometers back, by the stony rancor of the cross.

As the developing of a photograph in a darkroom slowly reveals the background, the figures, the colors of the negative being processed, or as the operation of reconstructing a palimpsest uncovers the blurred original writing beneath all the rest, so the progressive emptying of the dam is bringing to light the submerged universe whose flooding led to the tragedy of May 29, 1936. As the reservoir shrinks in size the water flow is reduced to a thin stream in the original beds of the rivers that feed it, and the meanders of the Tus wind in and out among what were once cultivated fields, today covered with dried, clay mud deposits. Here and there vestiges of dwellings stand out, the little bridge, still intact, along the old road, the bare ruins of the flour mill, the traces of a backcountry community that was suddenly wiped out. What before the construction of the dam were fertile plots of land along the riverside, the watercourses down which lumbermen once transported pine logs are reminders of the magnitude of the tragedy wrought by unemployment, domination by petty local political bosses, poverty, neglect on the part of the national government. The fierce repression that overtook Yeste and nearby districts in 1939 isolated its inhabitants inside a bell jar of reserve and silence that was to remain sealed for almost forty years. When I visited the town in 1963, people spoke in whispers of what had happened and silence was the only answer that my curious and naïve questions met with. As I had the occasion to learn myself not long after, they had every reason to be reserved.

The commemorative crosses escort rural route 3212 all the way to the entrance to the town. There, the economic take-off of the Sixties has appreciably modified the setting that exists in my memory: today's gas stations, bank branches, modern buildings, a spectacular increase in the number of cars. Unchanged, however, exactly as it is in my memory: the massive barracks of the Civil Guard.

To get a bird's eye view of Yeste, one must take the logging road that comes out at the Río Mundo and then winds its way up through a spectacular rugged panorama. The cypresses in the cemetery to the left are the ideal vantage point. The town curls round the foot of the looming bulk of the castle and the bell tower of the church stands out alone against the distant green of the mountainsides. In the whitewashed niches of the cemetery, stone tablets and inscriptions still commemorate the "glorious heroes fallen for God and Spain." Those who fell because they were rebelling against hunger, neglect, oppression that had gone on for hundreds of years are rotting, anonymous still, in the indignity of their common grave in a potter's field.

A kilometer farther on I recognize the curve in the road that was the scene of the massacre of peasants by the forces of law and order sent by the local political boss. The mouth of the conduit where the wounded took refuge, in which they were pitilessly finished off as they tried to crawl off toward the olive trees. The steep slope from which the Civil Guard fired on the multitude. No cross, no tablet commemorates the eighteen Spaniards who lost their lives among the pines, the bushes, and the brambles in this impressively wild setting. Heaven, prayers, posthumous glory continue to be the exclusive patrimony of those on whom fortune has smiled since their birth. The unbending will to stratification of our society lasts on into the next life.

Along the road down, splendid forests cover the foothills of the sierra and the visitor who has not returned for years spies to his left the frail little plank bridge that he crossed to reach the narrow winding dirt road that leads to the district of La Graya. The indomitable town from which the line of prisoners left that May day (they had been arrested for making charcoal in what had previously been communal property) has proudly survived decade after decade of severe trials, decimated first by the war, and thereafter the victim of the cruel privations of the depression. A fear that has been deep-rooted for so many years is not easily dispelled: according to the friend from the CNT labor union who is accompanying me as I do background research for an amateur documentary on the events recounted in my *Marks of Identity,* one of the few surviving witnesses of the slaughter fled to the mountains to avoid the questions that my friend and one of his comrades from the labor union wanted to ask him; the witness of this event of many years back apparently feared that if he were to recount his memories before the camera, the democratically elected provincial authorities would take away his modest old-age pension.

Nonetheless, five years after the death of the dictator, lips are beginning to become unsealed and the outsider no longer comes up against the wall of reserve that constantly brought him up short during his previous stay. In Yeste he was able to speak with a number of townspeople about the events of the 29th of May, of the wave of popular revenge the following summer, of the ultimate vengeance wrought by the rich and powerful classes once the Civil War was over. In Elche de la Sierra, during the running of the bulls, he had met the person who, under the pseudonym of Arturo, appears as a character in a few pages of his novel. The two of them had been denounced, no doubt by some kindly soul, and he had not been able to find out anything about "Arturo" since the day when the Civil Guard had interrogated them separately as to the content and purpose of their conversation and warned the outlander to get out of town immediately. He was finally able to learn Arturo's real name: Antonio López Sánchez, a member of the PSOE, the Spanish Socialist Workers' Party, since the days of the Republic, and today a scrap merchant in Hellín. Thanks to him, to his exemplary attitude, it had been possible in those difficult times for the writer to gather a series of extremely valuable data for his work.

During my travels through the Alcaraz and Ayna, Molinicos and La Bienservida, Letur and Ríxopar, one of the most beautiful and most unknown parts of the Peninsula, I was able yet again to note the vast discrepancy that exists between our urbano-industrial zones and the neglected and intractable rural universe. The political transformations of the country since Franco's death strike people in this latter world as remote and insignificant, like a mere vague rumor heard over television, without any real impact on their daily lives. Whereas the few bookstores that I found did not usually sell any of the democratic papers, Francoist dailies have no problems of distribution. The provincial offices of extreme right groups surpass, in showiness and numbers, those of the liberal postwar labor unions.

The standard of living of the towns has improved since the period when I wrote my novel, and people no doubt breathe more freely. But a simple glance at the politico-economic mechanism of control operating at present also clearly proves that the winning side in the war continues to exercise its traditional hold with as firm a hand as ever. Without intending in any way to reopen wounds or dig about in what remains—and must remain—hidden, I will nonetheless point out the incongruity inherent in the fact that in 1981 there still exist on the one hand inscriptions that are insulting to an entire town, such as the one I reproduce at the beginning of this article, while on the other hand no one speaks of the tragedy of dozens and dozens of families who dared rise up in arms and fight for ideals of freedom and justice that are part of our Constitution. Remaining silent about it even today is tantamount to stupidly perpetuating the abuses of a sinister past. If we Spaniards are not to fall into bitter factionalism once again, it is a past that each and every one of us must exorcise.

The Crime Committed in Port Bou

Just a few kilometers from the cemetery in Collioure where the poet Antonio Machado is buried, but on the other side of the border, the Spanish side, there is another cemetery, much less famous and less often visited, that Hannah Arendt describes in these words: ". . . it directly overlooks a cove on the Mediterranean; from a rocky ledge at the top, it descends in terraced steps, in whose stone walls the burial niches are set. It is undoubtedly one of the most extraordinary and most beautiful places that I have ever seen in my life."

The cemetery thus depicted is the one in Port Bou, painstakingly explored by the eminent Jewish writer in 1941 in a vain search for Walter Benjamin's grave. Though the seventy dollars Benjamin had with him on the day he died sufficed to pay the fee of the attending physician, the burial costs, and the acquisition of a vault for a period of five years, his friend could find no marker whatsoever of his gravesite. It was only many years later, long after the end of the war and long after the author of *A Berlin Childhood around 1900* had been rescued from the oblivion into which he had abruptly fallen, that a mysterious grave, surrounded by a wooden fence with his name scrawled on it, made its appearance; according to Gershom Scholem an outright fabrication by certain cemetery attendants who, on being frequently questioned by foreign visitors devoted to Benjamin's memory, had devised this clever stratagem to earn themselves tips. A typically Spanish reality, wherein so often craftiness and crime go hand in hand.

No one in Spain, so far as I know, has made any effort, even following the accession to power of a party with an anti-Fascist history, either to bring new light to bear on the facts in order to set the record straight once and for all, or to marshal public opinion in support of at least a symbolic gesture in payment of the reparation owed the victim. Even if we recognize the Hispanic penchant for the hocus-pocus of exhumations and the transfer of earthly remains—a necrophilian appetite that admittedly remained unsatisfied in the case of Don Antonio Machado "the Good"—the disappearing act which both Benjamin's mortal body and his memory have undergone is shocking. Neither the traditional blinkered ignorance of our cultural luminaries nor the lack of familiarity of the general public with the preoccupations and the life of this German thinker justifies such neglect and such silence. Spanish responsibility for a crime not all that different, in the last analysis,

67

from what happened in Granada[1] cannot be attributed solely to those who allowed it to take place: all of us share that responsibility. Benjamin's works belong to the common patrimony of European culture, and I for my part feel closer to his *oeuvre* than I do to that of the great majority of this country's writers.

Philosopher, essayist, traveler, Benjamin was first and foremost an exceptional cartographer of memory, a most discriminating explorer of the urban landscape, a keen-sighted, ever-curious forerunner of modernity. By way of his splendid evocations of his childhood, his fascination for great cities, his Parisian *flâneries* following in the footsteps of Baudelaire, his penetrating reflections on history and art, he staked out a territory of his own, vast and fraught with peril, through which today's reader roves in quest of plunder with the tense wariness, the thrill of excitement of a hunter on the prowl. A Marxist possessed of neither blind faith nor illusions, proscribed from his own country both as a Red and as a Jew, condemned to an uncertain, ever-wandering existence, he had found a temporary refuge in Republican Spain and there written sharp-sighted, animated pages on his stay in Ibiza. Many times, on re-reading him, I have pondered whether or not he had the presentiment, in one of those "pauses filled with silence" that reveal the seed of a "destiny very different from the one accorded us," of the one-way street, the blind alley into which the fanaticism and barbarity of his countrymen were inexorably driving him. As the catastrophe that obsessed him struck—world war, the Nazi invasion of France, hasty flight and precarious refuge in Marseille—the abundant testimony of his friends presents us with the picture of a clear-sighted, pessimistic man who, unlike his colleague Theodore Adorno, had let pass the chance to find shelter in the United States while there was still time and would appear to have suffered from a progressive loss of all his defense mechanisms, confronting events with a sort of free-floating, fatalistic anxiety.

Thanks to the letters and the detailed accounts of Lisa Fittko, Greta Freund, and the wife of Arkadi Burland, brought to light by Scholem and Rolf Tiedemann in their works on Benjamin, we are able to reconstruct, step by step, the itinerary—or better put, the calvary—of the writer from his arrival in Port Vendres with a small group of stateless persons to that cruel night of September 26, 1940 when, caught in the trap, he committed suicide in the hotel in Port Bou to which he had been taken by the police: the

---

[1] The reference is to the death of Federico García Lorca at the hands of a Francoist death squad in 1936, on the outbreak of the Spanish Civil War. (Trans.)

anxious wait for the arrival of the guide who was to show them the way to Spain; the human sympathy and aid of the mayor of Banyuls; the journey on foot to Cerbère with his black suitcase full of manuscripts; the reconnoitering, on the eve of the group's departure, of the path into Spain that they would be following; the sudden decision to spend the night up in the mountains instead of returning with the others to the town and starting out on the journey the next morning with them; the laborious ascent of the little band, through red-soiled vineyards suffused with luminous early-morning light; the writer's exhaustion, which threatened to bring on a heart attack at any moment; his anguished concern lest his manuscripts fall into the hands of the Gestapo; the euphoria that overcame the fugitives on catching sight of Port Bou.

What awaited them there has been described in precise detail by two personal participants in the drama: "At the Spanish border in Port Bou we went directly to the police so as to comply with the obligatory step of having an official entry stamp placed on our papers, but even though our travel documents were in order and we were in possession of Spanish transit visas, they categorically refused to stamp our papers. The chief of police maintained that he had just received new instructions from Madrid prohibiting those whose documents indicated that they were of "undetermined nationality" or "stateless" from entering Spanish territory. He insisted that we go back to where we had come from . . . and if we refused to obey his orders, he said that he would have us accompanied by an escort to a concentration camp in Figueras where we would be handed over to the German authorities." (Greta Freund, letter of October 9, 1940.) "For an hour, the three of us and four other women were overcome with despair, weeping and pleading with the authorities to whom we had shown our papers in good order. . . . They allowed us to spend the night in a hotel and introduced us to the three police officers who were to escort us to the frontier. . . . To Benjamin, being returned to France meant internment in a camp. . . . The following morning, around seven o'clock, Madame Lipmann sent word to me that he wanted to talk to me. Benjamin told me that the night before, at ten p.m., he had taken a massive dose of morphine, but that I should say that he was gravely ill. He gave me a letter for myself and another for Adorno. Then he lost consciousness. I alerted a doctor, but he managed to evade the responsibility of sending him on to the Figueras hospital in view of the fact that he was dying. I spent the rest of the day with the police, the mayor, and the judge, who examined Benjamin's papers and found among them a letter of recommendation to the Spanish Dominicans." (Madame Gurland, an account written on October 11, 1940.) The suicide of the author of *Paris, the Capital of the Nineteenth Century* saved the lives of the women who were with him: embarrassed and troubled by the scene they had made, the Francoist authorities allowed them to proceed on into Spain.

The naked cruelty of what had happened in this sinister border post raises a series of questions that we must face: Who was the chief of police who decided that Benjamin should be expelled from the country? What cause of death is listed in the doctor's certificate? What is recorded in the document drawn up by the magistrate who was sitting that day? Are these documents or any others preserved in the archives of that province? Is there no way to discover *pro memoria* the names of those parties who manifestly deserve a place in the universal history of infamy?

The manuscripts for which Benjamin was prepared to sacrifice his life disappeared along with all the rest of his belongings, and no one has ever been able to trace them: were they destroyed, handed over to the Gestapo, kept by the police? They are of inestimable value; do they not call for a rigorous investigation as to what happened to them? Is there a remote possibility that they could have been stored away somewhere and thus be brought to light again some day?

While we await answers to these questions, I shall pose others that address the principal issue even more directly: Is the beautiful Port Bou cemetery by the sea to be allowed to show visitors a fictitious tomb so as to hoodwink readers of Benjamin and line the pockets of gravediggers? Shouldn't German and Spanish democratic institutions make amends to this twofold victim of Hitler and of Franco? A bare, spare marker with the pure and simple setting forth of the facts, in the common charnel house in which he doubtless lies: would that not be the best remembrance of a man whose fruitful and stimulating thought continues, forty-four years after the crime, to leave its imprint on the greatest works of our time?

The Dillinger Museum

In a passage of my novel *Marks of Identity*, the protagonist, wandering through the streets of Geneva amid pompous, self-satisfied delegates to one of those congresses devoted to the fight against unemployment, war, disease, or underdevelopment that are a happy invention of the prosperous Swiss hotel industry, wondered why there were no congresses devoted to promoting the ruin and perdition of mankind, sponsored by the most notorious criminals of the century: Landru, Petiot, Giuliano, Dillinger, or Al Capone. Clearly, Álvaro Mendiola did not know that in the country that had contrived Disneyland his wishes had come true, or were about to, at least insofar as one of these famous malefactors is concerned: namely, John Dillinger.

Attendance at a meeting of Hispanists at a North American university can sometimes bring exquisite surprises. At the symposium on "The Spanish Novel Today," held in Bloomington, Indiana in September of 1980, the surprise element, although not totally lacking in cultural overtones, stemmed less from the literary debate itself than from the discovery of the existence of an exciting memorial museum located in Nashville, some eighteen miles away. The symposium of Hispanists not only brought together a group of friends scattered over two or three continents but also had, doubtless, its brilliant moments and memorable speeches. However, as is usually the case at this sort of colloquy, there were also a great many breaks, lulls, and moments that dragged, and worse still, the possibility of boring scholarly discourses or less than enjoyable encounters. Confronted with the threat of a paper on the narrative style of Castillo-Puche or a chance meeting during a coffee break with some learned stuffed shirt afflicted with halitosis, Jorge Edwards, Carlos Fuentes, Mario Vargas Llosa, and I opted for a change of air and the exploration of other more pleasing and instructive areas. Piloted by José Miguel Oviedo and Maryellen Bieder, we decided to satisfy our thirst for knowledge and fill the lacunae in our education by visiting the museum—though temple might be a better word if we take into account the respect and adoration of the numerous worshipers who enter its portals—commemorating a hero of my adolescence whom Zdanov and his commissars would surely not have categorized as *positive*.

I shall venture a terrible confession: museums make me ill. I have never been able to enter one without my eyes blurring, my head swimming, my mouth emitting cavernous yawns, and a sudden and invincible exhaustion causing excruciating pains in my back after only a few minutes. This malady is fairly common—the French call it *mal de musée*—and because of it, I systematically eliminate any artistico-cultural collection from my travel itinerary. After having seen dozens of Japanese tourists examining the Mona Lisa through dark glasses and polyglot groups of dazed sightseers perched on the Acropolis not knowing for certain whether the guide was about to recite the list of kings of the Goths to them or offer them a ride in a gondola, I have given up this sort of total immersion in knowledge, these massive doses of cultural pills that paradoxically produce in my mind precisely the opposite effect from that intended: the violent urge to make for the street and return to the world of the living. Though I am quite apt to board a train to go selectively admire a canvas by Hals, Goya, Titian, or Carpaccio, I flee general tours of the Prado, the Louvre, the Metropolitan, or the British Museum as I would the plague. If out of weakness or negligence I am trapped into such a visit, the sole artist of interest to me is the one labeled Uscita, Salida, Exit, Sortie, or Ausgang.

None of the symptoms of rejection—blurred vision, exhaustion, a splitting headache—troubled me in Nashville: after countless dull monuments to the glory of artists and exemplary citizens noted for their genius or their altruism, the mere reminder of a brief but dizzying existence devoted to evil and crime is tonic and refreshing. The feeling of delight is heightened if one also recalls the fact that the criminal in question did not triumph in his endeavor but, rather, came to grief in the most lamentable way: no veneer of subsequent social consideration attenuates the cruel reality of his career of crime. These factors, together with the nature of the place itself—small, unpretentious, built on a human scale—explain why the visit turned out to be, at least for me, as profitable as it was fascinating.

The Dillinger Museum is a modest house painted white, over the door of which—like the *Lasciate ogni speranza voi ch'entrate*—is a simple, irrefragable inscription: *Crime does not pay.* The building has two stories, and following an arrow through tiny but crowded rooms, the *aficionado* or the mere curious visitor may view a well-mounted exhibition of artifacts documenting the capital moments in the life of the town's most illustrious son: photographs of the hero and his cronies, from his childhood days to the apotheosis of his career; portraits of his victims, accomplices, and henchmen; newspaper writeups; family letters; police files and court records. Wax figures, armed with revolvers and submachine guns, reproduce his principal kidnappings and holdups. As in churches primarily dedicated to the worship of a particular virgin or saint, here too altars and lateral shrines evoke lesser luminaries, contemporaries of the star with top billing: Bonnie and Clyde, and a celebrated gunmoll whose name I do not remember at the moment. A synoptic table on the wall provides a chronology of the man whose memory is honored in this place: his date of birth, his grade-school studies, his travels, et cetera; a life that would appear to have been without problems, wreathed in a halo of *aurea mediocritas*. Then, coinciding with the Great Depression, there occurs that sudden break that Marxist disciples of Della Volpe call the *qualitative leap* and those of the German school the *Brusque Acceleration of History:* Dillinger holds up dozens of banks and post offices, stages daring robberies, murders a total of fourteen people.

And then, having thoroughly enjoyed himself, the visitor ascends to the second floor, where the ominous figure of the Lady in Red portends imminent tragedy; in order to keep from being deported, the sinister Roumanian *femme fatale* agrees to lure the demi-god into the ambush that is to cost him his life. When Dillinger falls to the sidewalk, riddled with bullets, just outside the movie theater where he has seen a film starring Myrna Loy and Clark Gable, Public Enemy Number One has in his pockets the modest sum of seven dollars. A glass case offers the faithful disciples and admirers of the gunman a view of carefully preserved relics: the straw hat, the glasses that shattered when he fell, the two ticket stubs to the movie, bloodstained garments. The sacrifice consummated, the public may examine a minutely detailed reconstruction of the autopsy; the hero's genitals, which were preserved—like the patriotic heart of Maciá, the first president of the Generalitat of Catalonia—in a jar of formaldehyde, are apparently kept at the headquarters of the F.B.I. in Washington, awaiting the moment when a generous fellowship from the Ford, the Guggenheim, or some other philanthropic foundation will permit some brilliant researcher to study them at his leisure for a master's or doctor's dissertation. The apotheosis: Dillinger lies on his catafalque, telling the beads of a Catholic rosary; to one side, on a little stand, is an underlined copy of the Bible. Press clippings of the period report that the country is plunged into ''national mourning'' on the day of the funeral; the family of the deceased receives thousands of telegrams of condolence and is offered solace by an immense crowd that accompanies it to the cemetery.

Unlike notorious smugglers or bandits promoted first to the rank of Knights of Industry and later to Patricians and Patrons of the Arts, Dillinger owes his status as a *sui generis* exemplary model to his failure. The museum in Nashville, Indiana serves us as a timely reminder that History is not made up of sublime deeds and glorious undertakings alone. As a necessary ingredient of society, evil too merits some form of recognition. Let us pay due tribute to the bold initiative of the city of Nashville in honoring the memory of this illustrious native son of the Hoosier State gone wrong, for it has thereby offered us a compensatory vision—in chiaroscuro, and hence more precise and complete—of the prodigious human adventure.

A Modest Proposal to the Princes of Our Wondrous Consumer Society

The sudden blackout that plunged more than ten million New Yorkers into darkness in July 1977 was described by the mass media of the entire world in dramatic and well-nigh apocalyptic terms: a night of terror, anguish, fires, robberies, aggression, pillage. The daily papers and mass-circulation news magazines devoted many column inches to nightmare scenes à la Hitchcock, images straight out of a futurist thriller, episodes from a sci-fi television serial. There is no denying that the panic, the violent rage and the despair of those store owners whose establishments were looted were real; it is equally true that for the space of a few hours, all notion of "civic conscience" disappeared in the poorest and most wretched areas of the city, and the law of the jungle held sway. But this manner of depicting what happened in a city that, willy-nilly, serves as the bellwether of all other world capitals— one needs only to observe, for instance, its insoluble and explosive set of interrelated problems to predict those that will sooner or later beset all the great cities of the so-called democratic world—neglects one important, significant, and unprecedented aspect of the event: the expansive, communal atmosphere of holiday rejoicing that reigned throughout the festivities among those oppressed classes and groups relegated to the margins of society.

Those of us who had occasion to watch on television scenes— some of them broadcast live—of what took place in Harlem, the Bronx, Jamaica, Williamsburg, Crown Heights, and Bedford-Stuyvesant discovered to our astonishment that thousands and thousands of blacks and Puerto Ricans—in the U.S. as in Europe, hair and skin color are the obvious indications of social differences—enjoyed an unexpected summer festival in which family and racial ties—neighborhood spirit—played an essential role. Groups of young people and adults smashed in display windows of stores and shops with planks, paving blocks, pickaxes, hammers, municipal garbage cans, urging each other on with chants and joyous cries: "Let's do it, let's do it!" Once the glass was broken, the door forced open, or the bars of the protective grille pried apart, the mob rushed in and through the openings, lighting their way with flashlights and, often, with rags or towels wrapped around their arms to keep them from getting cut by the broken glass, reappearing moments later with items of every sort, from the commonest and simplest to the most sophisticated and outlandish. Jewlery shops, groceries, clothing and appliance stores were visited by eager "customers" in a hurry and did a rousing business—all carry and no cash needed. Furniture stores were especially favored by a large clientele which, as if drawn by an irresistible hurricane of publicity, grabbed up all the bargains and clearance-sale merchandise in a shopping spree of unparalleled proportions: whole families made off with tables, armchairs, sofas, chests of drawers, living room suites, radios, television sets, mirrors, in an endless rush of traffic back and forth between stores and homes: two youngsters who couldn't have been over fifteen were seen pushing a giant-size refrigerator down the sidewalk; one couple was discovered carrying off a double or triple bed with all the accessories: feathering their nest, doubtless, for future cozy love-bouts. Supermarkets also did an extraordinary business: excited customers stuffed paper and plastic sacks full of produce, cans, bottles; others went directly out into the street with their shopping carts loaded with food and laughingly informed roving reporters that—in the words of one middle-aged woman wearing a turban and a pair of enormous sunglasses to conceal her identity—"It's a pleasure to go shopping without needing no fuckin' money!" Groups of kids picked out nice toys and pretty presents for themselves, rather than wait for what for them is the scarcely prodigal visit of Santa Claus or the Three Kings; adolescents of both sexes outfitted themselves with new shirts, shoes, and jeans, not to mention jackets and overcoats, in anticipation of the rigors of the coming winter. In the Bronx, people broke in the show window of a neighborhood car dealership and drove off fifty late-model Fords, Pontiacs, and Oldsmobiles, to go joyriding for a few hours with their girlfriends, relatives, or buddies, or to transport more readily the articles they had acquired in the gigantic, unexpected bargain sale. In short: strict hierarchization went by the board, marginality ceased to exist, and the individual felt like a human being again, amid other human beings.

For the space of a few hours the city ceased to be that implacable asphalt jungle in which the individual rots, suffers, and dies all alone in his ghetto and was transformed into a festive collectivity, a brotherhood of accomplices, all whooping it up together at that sudden super-party: members of an informal yet real association of frustrated customers, unjustly deprived until that moment of the right to satisfy a voracious consumer appetite stimulated by all the myriad publicity gimmicks of a system incapable, by reason of its scandalous social inequalities, of affording them adequate means to assuage it. As a policeman, speaking of those who had gone out on this "shopping binge," told the New York *Times*: "They couldn't understand why we were arresting them. They got really mad at us and kept saying: 'I'm out of a job and just taking what I need. Why the hell are you coming along to hassle me?'" A kid of eighteen or so, with a pair of pants "liberated" in some jeans store, explained to the same reporter from the *Times* that the revelers felt truly justified in view of the widespread unemployment and the depressed state of the economy: "Being out of work the way they are, they'd be really dumb not to do what they're doing."

What went on for nearly twenty hours after the blackout is, in my opinion, a revealing sign of the practically insoluble tensions that grip our consumer societies in the industrial countries—an incident that cannot be explained away, as might be naively supposed, as being merely another instance of the specific "monstrosity" of New York or even of the United States. These tensions are also a factor in the irremediable situation in which the great cities of Western Europe (Paris, Rome, London, Madrid, Barcelona, etc.) are little by little becoming trapped; in any one of them, each day more and more working-class families and marginal groups become the victims of the industrial fetishism and the pitiless exploitation of the bourgeoisie—workers and *lumpens* confronted, because of the recession, with the impossibility of selling even their miserable labor, and at the same time the helpless prey of consumer dreams whipped up night and day to a mad frenzy: stimuli which, by being endlessly repeated, create physical reflexes as effective and as immediate as those Pavlov discovered.

In the face of a dilemma of this magnitude, limiting ourselves, as the mayor of New York proposed, to a policy of stricter law enforcement and bigger police forces would be as useless as trying to cure a deadly infection with household remedies and mustard plasters. The danger that threatens the sacrosanct right to private property and a free-enterprise economy is much more profound and serious, and if we wish to safeguard these rights it is high time to take, as the saying goes, the bull by the horns. In view of the sad but demonstrated inability of the system to correct itself, to avoid cyclic depressions, and to do away with radical inequalities, I see only one solution, which I modestly propose to call to the attention of the civil, administrative, and municipal authorities of our countries whose consumer society is breaking down: extending and institutionalizing black-outs, requiring all cities of more than half a million inhabitants to have them, at the rate of one or two per year. Their date, obviously, must be kept secret; this could be done by means of a lottery in which a child, for example, chooses a number blindfold, whereupon the number is fed into a computer which, when the moment arrives—the H-hour indicated by the number drawn—goes into action and brings about the collapse of the entire electricity supply grid for the metropolitan area, thereby preserving—this is fundamental—the element of surprise. Poor citizens and disadvantaged classes would then know that it was "open season," and for a few hours they would have the right to procure whatever articles and consumer goods they required without the need for money, provided they managed to get around the protective devices that owners of commercial establishments naturally install, and provided they managed to stay out of the hands of the police. The latter, in turn, though, overwhelmed by events, would do their duty as best they could, endeavoring to come to the aid of owners whose stores were being visited and arresting a certain number of nocturnal looters. Possible rules of the game: strict prohibition of the use of firearms and, indeed, of any form of physical violence on the part of the revelers; kindliness and comprehension on the part of the forces of law and order; availability of an insurance policy to indemnify store owners against black-out losses. Advantages of this game: relaxing social tensions that might otherwise lead to a sudden uncontainable revolutionary explosion; compensating for the unfair distribution of goods by means of a festive free-for-all open to every class; permitting the indirect integration of the needy within the system, allowing them to have their fun and momentarily satisfying their consumer appetites. Other supplementary advantages: introducing an element of excitement into our dull daily lives; reviving the spirit of initiative and invention indispensable to a free-enterprise economy; making the social model more attractive to all its members; supplying bread and circuses to urban masses traditionally deprived of them. Not to mention the manna of an endless number of ancillary surprises: joyous, propitious promiscuity in the parks, offices, subway trains; the possibility of hopping, with no risk, into bed with one's neighbor; the pleasure of pinching whatever one feels like pinching, just for the fun of it.

If governments and municipalities of our democratic universe fail to realize the positive nature of the remedy proposed, they will beyond question be committing an extremely grave error: the preservation of the inviolable principles on which our industrial-consumer societies are founded depends on it. The alternative, I very much fear, would be a blowup infinitely more dangerous than a blackout.

Other Lumen Books

Under a Mantle of Stars
Manuel Puig
Translated by Ronald Christ

Culture and Politics in Nicaragua
Steven White

Sor Juana's Dream
Luis Harss

For an Architecture of Reality
Michael Benedikt

Dialogue in the Void: Beckett and Giacometti
Matti Megged